African Arguments

African Arguments is a series of short books about Africa today. Aimed at the growing number of students and general readers who want to know more about the continent, these books highlight many of the longer-term strategic as well as immediate political issues confronting the African continent. They will get to the heart of why Africa is the way it is and how it is changing. The books are scholarly but engaged, substantive as well as topical.

Titles already published

Julie Flint and Alex de Waal, *Darfur: A Short History of a Long War*

Tim Allen, *Trial Justice: The International Criminal Court and the Lord's Resistance Army*

Alex de Waal, *AIDS and Power: Why There is No Political Crisis – Yet*

Raymond W. Copson, *The United States in Africa: Bush Policy and Beyond*

Chris Alden, *China in Africa*

Tom Porteous, *Britain in Africa*

Julie Flint and Alex de Waal, *Darfur: A New History of a Long War*, revised and updated edition

Jonathan Glennie, *The Trouble with Aid: Why Less Could Mean More for Africa*

Peter Uvin, *Life after Violence: A People's Story of Burundi*

Bronwen Manby, *Struggles for Citizenship in Africa*

Camilla Toulmin, *Climate Change in Africa*

Forthcoming

James Boyce and Leonce Ndikumana, *Africa's Odious Debt*

Tim Allen, *Trial Justice: the Lord's Resistance Army, the Sudanese President and the International Criminal Court*, revised and updated edition

Orla Ryan, *Chocolate Nations: Living and Dying for Cocoa in West Africa*

Published by Zed Books and the IAI with the support of the following organizations:

InterAfrica Group The InterAfrica Group is the regional centre for dialogue on issues of development, democracy, conflict resolution and humanitarianism in the Horn of Africa. It was founded in 1988 and is based in Addis Ababa, and has programmes supporting democracy in Ethiopia and partnership with the African Union and IGAD. <www.sas.upenn.edu/African_Studies/ Hornet/menu_Intr_Afr.html>

International African Institute The International African Institute's principal aim is to promote scholarly understanding of Africa, notably its changing societies, cultures and languages. Founded in 1926 and based in London, it supports a range of seminars and publications including the journal *Africa*. <www.internationalafricaninstitute.org>

Justice Africa Justice Africa initiates and supports African civil society activities in support of peace, justice and democracy in Africa. Founded in 1999, it has a range of activities relating to peace in the Horn of Africa, HIV/AIDS and democracy, and the African Union. <www.justiceafrica.org>

Royal African Society Now more than a hundred years old, the Royal African Society today is Britain's leading organization promoting Africa's cause. Through its journal, *African Affairs*, and by organizing meetings, discussions and other activities, the society strengthens links between Africa and Britain and encourages understanding of Africa and its relations with the rest of the world. <www.royalafricansociety.org>

Social Science Research Council The Social Science Research Council brings much-needed expert knowledge to public issues. Founded in 1923 and based in New York, it brings together researchers, practitioners and policy-makers in every continent. <www.ssrc.org>

About the author

Camilla Toulmin is director of the International Institute for Environment and Development. An economist by training, she has worked mainly in Africa on agriculture, land, climate and livelihoods. This has combined field research, policy analysis and advocacy. Her work has aimed at understanding how environmental, economic and political change impact on people's lives, and how policy reform can bring real change on the ground.

CAMILLA TOULMIN

Climate change in Africa

Zed Books
LONDON | NEW YORK

in association with

International African Institute
Royal African Society
Social Science Research Council

FSC

Mixed Sources
Product group from well-managed
forests and other controlled sources

Cert no. SGS-COC-2953
www.fsc.org
© 1996 Forest Stewardship Council

Climate change in Africa was first published in association with the
International African Institute, the Royal African Society and the
Social Science Research Council in 2009 by Zed Books Ltd, 7 Cynthia
Street, London N1 9JF, UK and Room 400, 175 Fifth Avenue, New York,
NY 10010, USA

www.zedbooks.co.uk
www.internationalafricaninstitute.org
www.royalafricansociety.org
www.ssrc.org

Cover designed by Rogue Four Design
Set in OurType Arnhem and Futura Bold by Ewan Smith, London
Index: <ed.emery@thefreeuniversity.net>
Printed and bound in Great Britain by CPI Antony Rowe, Chippenham
and Eastbourne

Distributed in the USA exclusively by Palgrave Macmillan, a division
of St Martin's Press, LLC, 175 Fifth Avenue, New York, NY 10010, USA.

A catalogue record for this book is available from the British Library
US CIP data are available from the Library of Congress

ISBN 978 1 84813 014 2 hb
ISBN 978 1 84813 015 9 pb
ISBN 978 1 84813 461 4 eb

Contents

Tables, figures and boxes

Acknowledgements

This book originated in the request for me to give the Trapnell Lecture in Oxford in early 2007. Based on that lecture, I was asked to flesh out a book proposal for the series African Arguments. I am very grateful to Richard Dowden and Alex de Waal for persisting in pushing me to get it written, despite diverse distractions over the last two years. I have also drawn inspiration from each of their books, respectively *Africa: Altered States, Ordinary Miracles* and *Darfur: A New History of a Long War*, with Julie Flint.

I have benefited greatly, in writing this book, from the ideas and work of colleagues at IIED, and the extensive networks of people and organizations with which we have been linked for twenty years and more. These include networks on land tenure, decentralization, forest governance and pastoral development, as well as the work of the Climate Change Group at IIED, Capacity Strengthening of Least Developed Countries for Adaptation to Climate Change (CLACC), Up in Smoke?, and work on cities with Shack/Slum Dwellers International (SDI) and the Human Settlements Group at IIED. The institute, with its breadth of coverage and contacts, ensures that we think in multiple dimensions, and are challenged to articulate simple, clear messages about the need to bridge environment and development goals, while recognizing the huge diversity of settings.

Over the last twenty-five years, my regular visits back to a small village in central Mali have helped remind me of the enormous energy, initiative and adaptability of many people in Africa. Like all villages across the continent, it offers much instruction about change over time, and overturns many of the assumptions we bring to understanding people's goals and options. Many families in this small village, Dlonguebougou, have one foot in farming, and another in town, the hoe in one hand and a mobile phone in the other, with cooking still done on an open fire while a solar PV cell charges a battery for the radio. Seizing new opportunities and balancing the needs of individuals versus the collective interest are key elements in maintaining a successful domestic group in this drought-prone, high-risk environment. Ganiba Dembele has become a regular caller on his new mobile telephone and brings me up to date with village news. Sidiki Diarra and Yacouba Dème are faithful friends in Mali to whom I return again and again for help and advice.

Long-standing colleagues from IIED and before, such as Jeremy Swift, Gordon Conway, Ced Hesse, James Mayers, Duncan Macqueen, Saleemul Huq and Hannah Reid, have been very helpful in commenting on text and pointing me in new directions. Anna Wood provided a great deal of hard data collection and identification of key materials, helping me map out what needed to be covered in each chapter. Special thanks are due to her. Charlotte Forfieh, Liz Aspden and Simon Heawood have provided editorial help and assistance in formatting the chapters.

As I found it hard to set aside sufficient time for thought and writing during the working week, it was an enormous help to be given a yurt by friends Julian and Susie Leiper, in honour of our twenty-fifth wedding anniversary. The yurt was an excellent quiet place to which to retreat in the summer holidays of 2008. And, as always, special thanks to my husband Mark for giving me the space as well as casting an eagle editorial eye over chapters as they emerged.

Camilla Toulmin, London, April 2009

Abbreviations

ABN	Autorité du Bassin du Niger
AF	adaptation fund
AOSIS	Association of Small Island States
CDM	Clean Development Mechanism
CERs	Certified Emissions Reductions
CH_4	methane
CLACC	Capacity Strengthening of Least Developed Countries for Adaptation to Climate Change
CO_2	carbon dioxide
COP3	Third Conference of the Parties
COP13	Thirteenth Conference of the Parties
COP15	Fifteenth Conference of the Parties
ENSO	El Niño Southern Oscillation
ETS	European Emission Trading System
EU	European Union
GCM	General Circulation Models
GEF	Global Environment Facility
GHG	greenhouse gas(es)
HFCs	hydrofluorocarbons
IIED	International Institute for Environment and Development
IPCC	Intergovernmental Panel on Climate Change
ITCZ	Intertropical Convergence Zone
LDCs	Least Developed Countries
MDGs	Millennium Development Goals
N_2O	nitrous oxide
NAPA	National Adaptation Programme/Plan of Action
PFCs	perfluorocarbons
PRSPs	Poverty Reduction Strategy Papers

REDD	Reduced Emissions from Deforestation and Degradation
S_6F	sulphur hexafluoride
SDI	Shack/Slum Dwellers International
UNDP	United Nations Development Programme
UNEP	United Nations Environment Programme
UNFCCC	United Nations Framework Convention on Climate Change
WMO	World Meteorological Organization
WTO	World Trade Organization

1 | Introduction

The world's wealthiest countries have emitted more than their fair share of greenhouse gases. Resultant floods, droughts and other climate change impacts continue to fall disproportionately on the world's poorest people and countries, many of which are in Africa. (Archbishop Desmond Tutu)

Africa is the continent that will be hit hardest by climate change. Unpredictable rains and floods, prolonged droughts, subsequent crop failures and rapid desertification, among other signs of global warming, have in fact already begun to change the face of Africa. (Dr Wangari Muta Maathai, 2004 Nobel Peace Prize winner)

So finally today, there is an understanding that climate change is very real, it is happening and it is happening now. We can no longer consider it a threat that is yet to hit us; all over the world we see its impact. (Kofi Annan, opening address at the Global Humanitarian Forum, 2007)

Since 2006, climate change has become a major public issue. Everyone is talking about global warming, how to measure their carbon footprint, and whether it is still ethical to fly around the world. But what will climate change mean for different parts of the world – will some be winners and others losers? How will it affect the continent of Africa, and its many people who depend on farming or who have moved into its rapidly growing cities to find work, or whose incomes stem from the tourist economy? Will it hit rich and poor alike? And what kind of investment would help people and nations 'adapt' to climate change? Amid a rather sombre assessment of adverse impacts from global warming in many parts of the world, are there any opportunities that could bring better prospects for some peoples, such as the growth in financial markets for carbon? And if so, how might African people gain access to such markets?

We live in a world in which our global interconnectedness has become ever more evident, as shown by the extraordinary and unexpected hike in food and commodity prices from late 2006 to mid-2008. Biofuel targets set by the European Union (EU), the USA and China, among others, are part of the reason for the doubling or tripling of prices. Some observers have portrayed this as the rich world choosing to channel limited food supplies into generating fuel for gas-guzzling cars, rather than nourishing the world's poor. While there may be some truth in this, there are many other forces at work, such as the drought in Australia, growing demand for food from nations such as China and India, speculation in commodities, and the imposition of food export bans by a large number of countries, leading to further hoarding and price increases.

Like global warming, the global 'food crisis' demonstrates yet again that we live on a single planet where our decisions impact, whether we like it or not, on people often in distant parts of the world. In 1972, Barbara Ward, philosopher and writer, who founded IIED, the organization for which I work, wrote a prophetic book, *Only One Earth*, which laid out only too clearly the choices open to us then. These choices are even more pressing now. Thirty-seven years ago, she argued that we faced the real possibility, for the first time, of making the planet unfit for human life, and she took, as an example, the oceans, into which people tip a cocktail of wastes, as though they had boundless capacity to absorb whatever we empty into them. Second, she pointed to the impossibility of everyone on the planet living with the consumption levels of the rich world. But this then poses a difficult question: 'What is to be reduced, the luxuries of the rich or the necessities of the poor?' Third, she noted that there are many issues of huge planetary importance which cannot be solved by nations acting alone. 'The relentless pursuit of separate national interests by rich and poor alike can, in a totally interdependent biosphere, produce global disasters of irreversible environmental damage.'

Only One Earth was published half a lifetime ago, but the message is only too pertinent to our position today. The way we structure ourselves into families, neighbourhoods and nations may help us to mobilize energy and action to defend ourselves or pursue some great ambition, such as space travel. But in the face of global warming, regardless of which part of the world we inhabit, these tribal affiliations make no difference to our ability to protect ourselves and those we love. All will be affected in differing ways. This fundamental mismatch between the global span of the climate system and the social and political constructions within which we plan, make decisions and allocate resources presents a great challenge for our political leaders and the people they are meant to represent. The shortness of the electoral cycle, fear of telling the electorate that we have been living beyond our means, and the need to weigh our wants against the needs of both poor nations today and the rights of future generations tomorrow, together make for a complex manifesto for any political party. It is much easier to focus on tax cuts today and increased spending on health next week. Currently, our politicians are only tinkering at the margins, with a yawning gap between their proud claims to be addressing climate change on the one hand and the timid budgetary allocations that are dwarfed by more immediate political priorities. As Tom Burke reminds us, 'The problem is neither the economics nor the technology: it's the politics.' The credit crunch and the economic downturn offer a much-needed breathing space in which to rethink patterns of growth, ways of measuring progress and the means to build more resilient systems at global and local levels.

The Stern report, *Review of the Economics of Climate Change* (2006), commissioned by the UK government, showed that early action to cut emissions of greenhouse gases (GHG) makes much more sense than waiting for another decade or two and then trying to adapt to the consequences. This is partly because there are time lags in the global climate system, which mean that, even were we to be successful in cutting emissions to zero today, another twenty to thirty years of warming are inevitable. The rising concentration of GHG in the atmosphere will bring ever rising global temperatures,

3

as described in more detail in Chapter 2. The longer we leave the cutbacks in GHG, the bigger the rise in temperature, the larger the adverse impacts and the more costly it will be to bring down emissions. Stern argues we should start now to make the necessary investments over a period of time which will lead us to a low-carbon economy at a manageable pace. We cannot afford to wait and risk the uncertain and potentially catastrophic impacts of climate change (Stern 2009).

Scientists can only give us a range of predictions on how different GHG concentrations will feed into higher temperatures, because of the difficulty of modelling the complex systems that make up the different levels of the atmosphere and its interlinkages with land and sea. There are also some concerns that global warming may feed back into further accelerating the rise in GHG and temperatures. These include the possibility of the methane currently trapped in the frozen Siberian tundra being released as northern Russia starts to warm up. This tundra is estimated to contain 70 billion tons of methane. If even a small fraction of this escapes, it will eclipse the estimated 600 million metric tons of methane that are emitted each year, from natural and human sources, and cause a dramatic acceleration in global warming. Equally, as the world warms, there will be limits to how much CO_2 can be absorbed by the soils and oceans. Normally, land and water act as a 'sink' by absorbing CO_2 from the atmosphere but, with rising temperature, these sinks may start to act as 'sources', releasing rather than absorbing GHG.

This book outlines what research tells us about the likely impacts of global warming on the African continent. Written for a mainstream audience, it tries to avoid technical language and argument, while recognizing the uncertainties inherent in modelling global climate systems and predicting how they play out on the ground. It starts from a recognition that, while no body of science can provide all the answers, the college of scientists in the Intergovernmental Panel on Climate Change constitutes the best foundation for understanding what is happening to the world's climate. Set up in 1988, the IPCC prepares an assessment of knowledge about climate change every four to five years, drawing on existing peer-reviewed literature. The fourth and latest IPCC assessment report dates from 2007 and concludes for the first time that the evidence of man-made global warming, linked to emissions of GHG, is now incontrovertible. Because the IPCC works on the published literature, it is inevitably working with material that is two to three years old. Scientific evidence emerging over the last two years indicates that the process of global warming is happening faster than the IPCC report suggests, and global emissions of GHG are even higher than the most pessimistic of the scenarios outlined in the report. While one or two climate sceptics describe the IPCC as alarmist, much well-informed opinion worries that – in their attempt to be cautious in their interpretation of the evidence – the IPCC's fourth and latest assessment report underestimates the risks of runaway global climate change we now face.

The year 2009 is a critical period for making progress in addressing climate change, with the hope that agreement will be reached on a new global treaty at the Copenhagen climate conference in December. As a successor to the current Kyoto protocol, which runs out in 2012, this treaty will need to establish new and more binding targets for cutbacks to GHG among rich countries. It will need to offer a variety of options for helping other countries, such as India, China and Brazil, move to a pattern of economic growth that minimizes their GHG emissions in future. Science tells us that global emissions of GHG need to fall by at least 50 per cent by 2050, in comparison with 1990 levels, if we are to limit the risk of dangerous climate change. Developed countries will need to commit to cutting emissions by 80–90 per cent by 2050 in comparison with the 1990 baseline. Developing countries with major emissions, such as China, India, South Africa and Brazil, will need to set targets in advance of 2020, if global emissions are to peak and then fall in time. Such long-term targets and credible interim goals will help firm up the price to be paid for carbon reductions, which will act as a strong, positive incentive for a wide range of new technologies. Stern (2009) outlines a number of other elements that would need to form part of the deal, which include developed countries demonstrating that they can achieve low-carbon growth and provide resources and technologies to developing countries to help them follow suit, offering a cost-effective means of reducing deforestation, and supporting vulnerable countries in adapting to the impacts of climate change.

It is hoped that the Copenhagen summit will produce a text along these lines, but most observers recognize that we are currently a long way from reaching an agreement of this sort. The election of Barack Obama as US president offers much greater hope of progress in reaching a climate agreement, given his statements and the appointment of serious scientific advisers in his administration. The high price for oil and gas up to mid-2008 brought about a significant cutback in demand for big cars and made renewable energy sources much more competitive. These trends have now been reversed, however, given the collapse in oil prices and financial difficulties facing investors. The growth in carbon markets has established a mechanism for seeking out carbon emission reductions in different sectors, and different regions of the world. This has generated a new constituency of interests in obtaining a successful post-Kyoto treaty, which can start to provide a counterweight to the very powerful set of vested interests linked to the fossil fuel economy.

On the other side of the coin is the lack of ambition from politicians and governments. European governments, which see themselves as at the progressive end of the climate change negotiations, are still far behind what many businesses and citizen groups would like to see achieved in terms of emission cuts. The global credit crunch and economic slowdown in North America and Europe have increased budget deficits, and have made people feel poorer and more vulnerable, while the breakdown of the WTO negotiations has sent out a signal that many governments are more interested in narrow domestic interests than gaining an equitable global agreement. Climate sceptics have been sowing the seeds of doubt, pandering to the self-interest of those who want no change in current arrangements. Globally, our economies remain firmly wedded to oil and gas as the fuels that keep our economies working and growing, with all the associated infrastructure of refineries, pipelines and road systems. The big oil and gas giants, eight of which are among the top twenty publicly quoted companies, are powerful actors able to lobby for their interests at national and global levels. Oil-producing countries and companies have a very strong interest in maintaining the status quo of the fossil fuel economy, and ensuring a return on their continuing investment in the steel and concrete needed to service the extraction, processing and distribution of oil.

Where does the African continent sit in relation to these global trends and debates? In some ways, the diversity to be found within Africa's landmass and its enormous size make generalizations impossible. With a surface area of 30 million square kilometres, Africa is seven times larger than the current EU and three times the size of China. But despite this evident diversity in people and place, there are some important common features, including continued heavy reliance on natural resources and agriculture, low levels of income per head, and consequent marginalization in global political affairs. With high levels of inequality, and limited government capacity to deliver services to the majority of people, many states serve the interests of an elite, especially where mineral or oil wealth generates significant riches. Apart from the North African region and South Africa, there has been limited industrialization, and even this is threatened by the huge strength of the Chinese manufacturing sector, with its capacity to produce enormous volumes of low-price goods. Hence, in terms of the world economy, African countries remain largely a source of raw materials and agricultural commodities.

As regards climate change, Africa also stands out as the continent that has contributed the least amount of greenhouse gases to the atmosphere in terms of current flows and existing stocks. For example, for 2007, which is the most recent year for which full data are available, per-head emissions of CO_2 for all of Africa stood at 1 tCO_2 (tonnes of CO_2), in comparison with a world average of 4.3 tCO_2, a US figure of 19.9 tCO_2, the EU15 (the fifteen countries in the EU at the start of 2004) with 6.9 tCO_2 and China

One

with 3.2 tCO$_2$. South Africa is the one exception, with an average of 7.9 tCO$_2$/person in 2004 (UNDP 2007/08), a level very similar to that of high-income countries. This is due to the very high reliance on coal for electricity generation.

In terms of the historic responsibility for GHG in the atmosphere, Africa is even more starkly at odds with the rest of the world, having contributed 2.3 per cent of CO$_2$ emissions by 2004 in comparison with 11 per cent for the EU15, 20.9 per cent for the USA and 17.3 per cent for China. In a fair world, in which all people have equal rights to the atmosphere, this should mean that Africa has considerable rights to emit, which have not yet been exercised. But one of the perversities of the climate change negotiations is that it is the big emitters who exercise power – the USA, the EU, China, India and Brazil. It is they who can hold the rest of the world to ransom, by quibbling over 5 or 10 per cent targets, or by trying to shift the calculation of target reductions from a 1990 baseline to one more accommodating of their interests, such as 2008.

Those people who are most likely to be hardest hit by global warming have little or no voice, since they have nothing to trade. In the past, African countries have been forced to 'take' whatever agreements and rules are established by world leaders, rather than having a seat at the table at which the rules are made. The Copenhagen talks are likely to be no different. Africa's weak economic position is one reason, and its diversity is another. With a rising number of oil- and gas-producing nations, as well as some of the poorest countries, their interests are too divergent for them to speak with a common voice. And within many countries, inequalities in political power and economic interests between the rich elite and the poor majority mean that the needs and perspectives of millions of small-scale producers are not well represented by governments when it comes to negotiations. In more extreme cases, the rich have bank accounts offshore and family members elsewhere in the global diaspora, allowing them an alternative future when things get bad at home. The poor have few if any options, except risking the sea crossing in a leaky fishing boat from Senegal, Libya or Morocco, in the hope of a landfall in Europe. While the

Kyoto protocol, agreed in 1997, has established a range of new financial opportunities to sell carbon emission reductions, through the EU's Emission Trading System and the Clean Development Mechanism, African nations have had only a very small slice of the pie. Those seeking to buy such carbon reductions find it much easier going to major polluters, such as India, China and Brazil, where they can do deals with a few large industrial enterprises, rather than many small-scale producers, given the costs of pooling a large number of small transactions. Equally, buyers of carbon feel more secure in their purchases where there is greater certainty about contracts, and land and property rights.

Global justice, ethics and human rights

As Barbara Ward made clear in *Only One Earth*, our continued existence on this planet depends on us understanding what our global interconnectedness means, and shifting our behaviour towards a more sustainable use of the earth's finite resources. This will have to involve a fairer way of dividing up those things that are most scarce. Between 1972 and today, we have seen a big shift in understanding of where the greatest scarcity lies. When the Club of Rome produced its report *Limits to Growth* (Meadows et al. 1972), they highlighted the risks of running out of natural resources, such as metals, fossil fuels and water, but paid little attention to global warming. Today, many new oil and gas reserves are being discovered, such as off the coast of Brazil in seas thousands of metres deep. With each year's melting of the Arctic ice cap, further quantities become accessible to be exploited by the rush of neighbouring countries laying claim to mining rights.

In contrast to the Club of Rome's report, it is now clear that the scarcest resource is the capacity of our atmosphere to continue to absorb the growing volume of CO_2 and other GHG that we generate. How should we allocate this scarce resource? Should it be on the basis of where we are now, which confirms the status quo and the associated power of the big polluters? Or should we opt for a fairer, more radical approach, in which all people around the world are deemed to have an equal stake in the atmosphere, and hence rights in and responsibilities for the future of our planet? This is the key principle underlying 'Contraction and Convergence' and a number of other proposals for managing global warming. In the current global setting, is it better to pitch high for an equity-based solution, or go for the second best, which is more in tune with the current power balance?

The political philosopher John Rawls outlined a theory of distributive justice, which sought to promote 'justice as fairness'. He argued that people are likely to develop the ideal set of rules and institutions if they start from a point where no rules currently exist – a situation Rawls calls the 'original position' – and with the goal that any new rules are based on equal basic liberties for all. The rules will also be fairest if they are drafted by people acting as though they are behind a 'veil of ignorance' and do not yet know where they will be in the future economic and political hierarchy. Rawls's hypothesis is that by applying these principles, people are likely to construct a society based on rules that deliver the best possible outcome for everyone.

Let us take an analogy familiar to many parents. Suppose we are at a child's birthday tea party and, having blown out the candles, the birthday girl or boy is given the job of cutting the cake and handing out slices to the eager faces around the table. Her first inclination might be to cut and take a large piece first and then let the other children scramble for slices of their own. But if a wise mother or father suggests the birthday child take their piece last, out comes a protractor to ensure that a completely fair division of the cake is achieved, so that whether any child is first or last makes no difference to how much they get.

At present the rules for addressing climate change are being written by the powerful and polluting nations. And it is inevitable that the deal they reach among themselves will pay particular attention to their current and future interests. It is as if the birthday cake is being devoured by a few special friends, while the rest of the party must sit and watch, hoping for a few crumbs left on the plate. It would be fairer for the post-Kyoto treaty to be written by those at the bottom of the global hierarchy with nothing to trade but most to lose from the current way of doing business. A grouping of the poorest 100 nations, or some combination of the Association of Small Island States (AOSIS), or the fifty-three Least Developed Countries (LDCs) – many of which are in Africa – would craft a very different kind of text and associated rules. These groupings need to gain a much louder, stronger voice in the ongoing negotiations for the Copenhagen agreement, and to become better able to represent the interests of those who are politically marginal within their own countries, by listening to the perspectives of slum dwellers, herders, farmers and forest peoples – women, men, poor and better off – across their respective nations.

This book outlines the likely consequences of climate change for different parts of Africa and different sectors. It recognizes that climate change is only one of many powerful forces affecting African development prospects, both internal and external. It starts, in Chapter 2, with a review of what the science predicts as regards the impacts of global warming, what this means for different regions of the African continent, and the evidence of change in temperature and rainfall to date. It describes the international institutions charged with addressing climate change, and the timetable for negotiations, before examining the scales at which adaptation to climate change needs to take place. Chapter 3 covers how global warming affects water availability, with some areas becoming much drier and others considerably wetter. Overall, there is the prospect of more frequent extreme weather events, such as drought, floods and storms, as heating of the global atmosphere drives a more active and moisture-laden weather system. The exceptional floods that hit many parts of Africa in September 2007 are a reminder that too much water can be a problem, as well as too little. This chapter also looks at the very limited investment made to date in managing water supply for people's domestic needs, whether in villages or big cities, as well as the untapped potential for both small and larger dams to capture water for energy generation and agricultural production. Such investments, however, need to keep in mind future projections of water availability, and what this means for river flows.

Food systems are the subject of Chapter 4, which outlines the great reliance of most countries on agriculture and natural resources. Given the likely rise in temperatures and shifts in rainfall, many farmers will face yet more challenging growing conditions. Livestock production may do somewhat better than crops, especially if a shift is made away from cattle, which are less heat tolerant, and towards goats, sheep and camels, which are better able to cope in drier, hotter conditions. Changes in climate will also affect inland and coastal fisheries, and the myriad wild foods that give a harvest of great value to many rural people. The chapter finishes with a look at how greater resilience can be incorporated into farming systems, building on experience from the West African Sahel.

Chapter 5 deals with forests, and their enormously important role as a local source of income and provider of services, as a national economic asset and as a global resource essential to the maintenance of our global climate system. We know little as yet about how forests may themselves be affected by changes in temperature and rainfall, but we do know they are key to the global carbon cycle, with the Congo Basin second only to the Amazon in size and importance. It is not only tropical wet forests which provide incomes and ecological services. In the extensive drylands of Africa, trees play a vital role as a source of fruit, fodder and fuel, as well as giving shade and helping stem erosion, by cutting wind speeds. With the growth in carbon markets, questions arise about who actually owns the rights to trees in different parts of Africa and, hence, who can claim the payments from a global fund to provide cash in compensation for avoided deforestation.

Cities are the subject of Chapter 6. The development business has largely neglected cities in Africa, despite their accommodating 30–50 per cent of the population in many parts of the continent. The growth of towns and cities has been seen as a problem, rather than a sign of economic growth and diversification. This chapter examines how many of Africa's big cities and smaller towns may be affected by climate change, and how they might adapt to such changes. It highlights the need for city governments and urban councils to work more closely with residents' associations, neighbourhood leaders and community groups to design together ways of handling shifts in water supply, risks of flooding and increased vulnerability to hazards. It also looks at the potential for cities to be part of the solution to climate change, through their redesign to deliver low-carbon growth in ways that benefit, rather than exclude, the poor majority.

Some of the more apocalyptic writers on climate change emphasize the likelihood of conflict over increasingly scarce resources, such as water, food and land. Chapter 7 assesses the evidence for these views to date, whether we are already seeing the first 'climate change wars' and what might be done to reduce the risks of shifts in resource availability generating devastating conflict. It concludes that the reasons for war are usually independent of an environmental challenge, such as climate change, and one should be cautious in inferring a simple relationship between increased scarcity and fighting. It is clear, however, that the more catastrophic predictions of temperature rises and rainfall failures could unleash major shortfalls in food and water and political upheaval in many regions.

Chapter 8 opens up discussion of what different African countries might gain or lose from a 'low-carbon economy' in which the sale of carbon services forms an ever larger source of income. Examples include payments for avoided deforestation, and the growth in biofuel production. As noted earlier, African countries have found it difficult to get their voices heard at the global decision-making tables, which design the markets and rules for access. African countries' ability to gain from the emerging carbon economy depends very much on making sure their perspectives and interests are built in from the start. This means getting centrally involved in negotiations over the next two to three years, during which new mechanisms and institutions will be designed to deliver a global economic system which can continue to grow in delivery of goods and services in ways that dramatically bring down the levels of GHG associated in their production, distribution and consumption. The final chapter looks forward to the challenges climate change poses for the world as a whole, the scale of response required, and the practical and political hurdles faced.

At the Copenhagen summit and beyond, there is much work to be done in the rich world to alert people to the very real risks we run of global warming creating a planet 'unfit for life', and to our particular responsibility for the stock of GHG in the atmosphere, which is forcing a different pattern of economic growth on us all, if we are to avert disaster. African countries have had very little part in generating the problem we now face, and have had no voice in designing solutions, which should meet the needs not only of the big GHG polluters, but also the many parts of the world that will feel major impacts. It will be vital to get the perspectives of African citizens into the current negotiation process, so that their experience, knowledge and worries can weave as threads through the fabric of the texts to be agreed. As Barbara Ward reminds us, we face a clear and simple choice – will we design a world that preserves the way of life of the rich, or addresses the urgent needs of the poor? The choice is ours.

2 | Global climate change and Africa

Introduction

This chapter presents an overview of climate change science and the implications of the IPCC's assessment report of 2007 for different regions of Africa. It outlines the global architecture of agreements, institutions and funding mechanisms set up to address the problem, and reviews performance in achieving cuts in greenhouse gas emissions. For most African countries, given their low level of emissions per head, the climate change challenge is mainly one of finding ways to adapt to the range of impacts now considered inevitable. Adaptation needs attention at multiple levels, combining a focus on building more resilient local food and water systems with national plans for food security and international management of key resources, such as river basins.

Given our current state of knowledge, no region of Africa looks like being a winner from global warming. This is because nowhere in Africa does low temperature act as a constraint on growing conditions, except in a very small number of high mountain regions. Even where rainfall increases, much of this is expected to be in heavier and more torrential conditions, leading to increased run-off and erosion. This stands in contrast to some other regions of the world, which may experience gains from global warming in the next twenty to thirty years, such as more favourable farming conditions in some parts of Russia and Canada.

Background to climate change

It has been over one hundred years since the Swedish scientist, Svante Arrhenius, along with Thomas Chamberlin, calculated that human activities could warm the earth by adding carbon dioxide. At the time of the first UN Conference on the Human Environment, held in Stockholm in 1972, there was some acknowledgement of climate change as a possible problem, but most environmental research was concerned with limits to growth caused by our running out of key natural resources such as oil, and the pollution of others such as water and land.

It was not until 1988 that the Intergovernmental Panel on Climate Change was set up to assess and synthesize the latest scientific, technical and socio-economic literature on global warming. It operates under the auspices of the World Meteorological Organization (WMO) and the United Nations Environment Programme (UNEP). The IPCC does not carry out research, but collaborates with hundreds of scientists and experts throughout the world, as well as governments. It has produced four Assessment Reports to date, in 1990, 1995, 2001 and 2007. Owing to the highly political nature of global debate on climate change, the IPCC has been very careful to maintain a strictly neutral position as regards policy prescriptions, such care and authority being rewarded in 2007 by joint nomination along with Al Gore for the Nobel Peace Prize.

The IPCC's latest report (2007) states: 'Warming of the climate system is unequivocal, as is now evident from observations of increases in global average air and ocean temperatures, widespread melting of snow and ice and rising global average sea level' (IPCC 2007). Concerning Africa directly: 'Africa is one of the most vulnerable continents to climate change and climate variability, a situation aggravated by the interaction of "multiple stresses", occurring at various levels, and low adaptive capacity. Changes in a variety of ecosystems are already being detected, particularly in southern African ecosystems, at a faster rate than anticipated' (Boko et al. 2007). Given its publication date of early 2007, much of the evidence on which the report was drawn up came from published material over the period 2000–05. Since 2005, there has been an ever larger body of scientific observation that shows the world is warming faster than the models used by the IPCC suggest (Pile et al. 2008).

The causes of climate change – an overview

The earth's climate is determined by a combination of the energy we receive from the sun and the physical and chemical properties of the earth's surface and atmosphere. Some of the sun's radiation striking the earth is absorbed by the surface, while the rest is reflected, either escaping into space or becoming trapped by gases in the earth's atmosphere. Trapped radiation is then recycled back to earth, adding extra warmth to the surface – a process called the 'greenhouse effect'. This is a natural phenomenon that ensures that the amount of energy coming in is balanced by that radiated into space, so maintaining a relatively stable temperature at the earth's surface. The concern over global warming focuses on gases in the earth's atmosphere, which have a capacity to absorb the radiation reflected from the earth, so trapping heat. Most greenhouse gases (GHG), such as carbon dioxide (CO_2) and methane (CH_4), occur naturally, and are normally present at atmospheric concentrations that effectively regulate the earth's temperature. An increase in their concentration has occurred over the last 250 years, however, due to human activities, such as burning carbon-based fuels – an increase which has intensified the greenhouse effect and is leading to global warming. Other greenhouse gases, such as nitrous oxide (N_2O), are man-made and are also increasing in concentration. The increase in man-made GHG has also been accompanied by an increase in small particles of dust, soot or sulphur from industrial pollution and soil erosion, which reflect or absorb incoming solar radiation, also leading to cooler or warmer conditions. Volcanic eruptions are a very important source of such particles and play a part in global cooling.

The world's atmosphere and climate – a situation report

Some examples of the evidence:

• The concentration of atmospheric CO_2 has increased from a pre-industrial value of about 280 ppm in 1750 to 379 ppm in 2005. This is compared to an increase of only 20 ppm over the 8,000 years prior to industrialization. Concentrations of GHG are currently at 430 ppm of CO_2 equivalent.[1] A level of 550 ppm could be reached by 2035, and at this level there is a 77–99 per cent chance that global average temperature rise will exceed 2°C.

• Taking all emissions since 1750 to date, Europe and North

America have contributed the greatest amount of CO_2 in the atmosphere, but more recently China has become the single largest generator of GHG. Africa, by contrast, has generated only a very minor share of GHG.

• Since 1750, about two-thirds of man-made CO_2 emissions have come from fossil fuel burning and about one-third from land use change. About 45 per cent of this CO_2 has remained in the atmosphere, while about 30 per cent has been taken up by the oceans and the remainder by soils and vegetation.

• The years 2005 and 1998 were the warmest since records began in 1850. Surface temperatures in 1998 were enhanced by the major 1997/98 El Niño event, but no such anomaly was present in 2005. Eleven of the twelve years 1995 to 2006 rank among the twelve warmest years on record since 1850.

• There has been a substantial increase in heavy rainfall events, even in those regions where there has been a reduction in total rainfall.

• Heatwaves have increased in duration since the latter half of the twentieth century. The record-breaking heatwave over western and central Europe in the summer of 2003 is an example of a recent extreme event. The summer months of June, July and August in 2003 were the warmest since comparable records began around 1780.

• Over the 1961 to 2003 period, global mean sea level rose by 1.8 $\pm$ 0.5 mm per year, owing largely to the expansion of seawater as it warmed. This expansion will contribute to sea level rise over the next 100 years, even if atmospheric concentrations of greenhouse gases are stabilized at current levels. Adding water from melting ice caps and glaciers will raise the sea level by more than 1 metre by 2100.

The UN Framework Convention on Climate Change and the Kyoto protocol

In 1992, at the Earth Summit in Rio, most countries of the world adopted a new international treaty called the United Nations Framework Convention on Climate Change (UNFCCC). This was a major step in acknowledging the dangers of global warming. As GHG emission levels continued to rise around the world, it became evident that a further commitment to reduce emissions was needed, through negotiation of a protocol. After intense negotiations, the Kyoto protocol was developed and adopted in 1997 during the third annual Conference of the Parties (COP3) to the UNFCCC. Following ratification by most developed countries, and finally by Russia, the Kyoto protocol entered into force on 16 February 2005 and in its current form runs until 2012.[2] Some countries, however, have not ratified the Kyoto protocol, of which the USA is the most notable. After years of failing to ratify the treaty, the incoming Australian government headed by Kevin Rudd made it one of its first acts to adopt the protocol in November 2007, enabling it to take part in the Bali climate negotiations in December 2007, the thirteenth annual Conference of the Parties to the UNFCCC (COP13).

Negotiations are now under way for a successor to the Kyoto treaty, to be operational from 2012 onwards. It is hoped that such a treaty might be agreed at COP15, due to be held in Copenhagen in December 2009. Barack Obama, as the new US president, has committed his administration to negotiating a global agreement along similar lines to those being proposed by the European Union.

The UNFCCC distinguishes between Annex 1 and non-Annex 1 countries. The former comprise richer developed countries, which have agreed to reduce their GHG emissions over the period from 2008 to 2012. The targets adopted by each Annex 1 country add up to a total cut in GHG emissions of at least 5 per cent against the baseline of 1990. Review and enforcement of these commitments are carried out by United Nations-based bodies. The six main greenhouse gases covered by the treaty are carbon dioxide (CO_2); methane (CH_4); nitrous oxide (N_2O); hydrofluorocarbons (HFCs); perfluorocarbons (PFCs); and sulphur hexafluoride (S_6F), with the limits of each being measured in equivalents of carbon dioxide.

The targets for cuts in greenhouse gases to be enshrined in the post-Kyoto treaty to come into force in 2012 will need to be ambitious, given that scientists now tell us that warming is happening at a faster rate than predicted. Many European countries

19

have signed up to a cut in emissions of 60–80 per cent by 2050, with a range of intermediate targets. For example, the EU has announced a 20–30 per cent cut by 2020, and the USA under the new administration is expected to follow a broadly similar track. These cuts are relative to the 1990 baseline established under the Kyoto protocol.

Progress in meeting these earlier targets has been disappointing, with few Annex 1 countries actually achieving them. Where these targets have been reached, such as by the UK, it is in large part because we have outsourced our emissions to China, which now manufactures many of the products that formerly were made domestically. Those countries such as Denmark and Norway which have not reached their targets through domestic cuts will meet their commitments through purchase of credits on the carbon market.

It is expected that the major emerging economies of China, India and Brazil will also take on targets of some sort, given the scale of their emissions and the urgency of the problem. The main questions concern what these targets might comprise, when they would become binding, and the financial assistance sought to shift to a low-carbon economy.

All African countries are signatories to the UNFCCC and, as they are non-Annex 1 countries, there is no cap on their greenhouse gas emissions under the Kyoto protocol, which places a larger burden on developed nations under the principle of 'common but differentiated responsibilities'. This has two grounds. First, richer countries can more easily pay the cost of cutting emissions, and second, developed countries have historically contributed much more to the problem by emitting more GHG per person than developing countries.[3]

In order to give developed countries a degree of flexibility in meeting their emission reduction targets, the protocol has developed several market-based mechanisms to facilitate reductions, which involve the trading of emissions through systems such as the European Emission Trading System (ETS) and the Clean Development Mechanism (CDM) (Crosby et al. 2007). The CDM provides

TABLE 2.1 Clean Development Mechanism projects registered by region (data for February 2009)[4]

Region	Number of projects	Percentage of total
Africa	29	2
Asia and the Pacific	973	69
Latin America and the Caribbean	396	28
Other	8	1
TOTAL	1,406	100

for industrialized countries to implement projects that reduce GHG emissions in developing countries in return for Certified Emissions Reductions (CERs) that can be used to help meet a fraction of their own obligations. CDM is the one means by which developing countries are involved in the implementation of the protocol.

These mechanisms are meant to help identify the lowest-cost opportunities for reducing emissions and attract private sector involvement. For example, developing nations can benefit in terms of technology transfer and investment brought about through collaboration with industrialized nations under the CDM. The credits accrued through these projects by developed countries go towards meeting their emissions commitments. To date, however, Africa has been relatively poorly served by the CDM (see Table 2.1 above). The reasons for this are that many of the cheapest means of reducing GHG emissions can be found in large-scale industrial enterprises in countries like China and India, where a new piece of technology can prevent the escape of large amounts of GHG. African countries suffer from not having been large enough polluters to benefit from a mechanism like the CDM. The transaction costs of putting together a CDM project and getting it certified are also very high, so that it is only large-scale projects which are worth taking forward.

As will be seen in Chapter 8, there are other potential opportunities for African countries to engage in carbon finance outside the CDM, where transaction costs are considerably lower. These

TABLE 2.2 Regional temperature and rainfall projections for 1980/99 to 2080/99

Region	Median projected temperature increase (°C)	Median projected rainfall change (%)	Level of agreement on rainfall estimates, by months of the year
West Africa	3.3	+2	Not strong
East Africa	3.2	+7	Strong for increase in DJF, MAM and SON
Southern Africa	3.4	−4	Strong for decrease in JJA and SON
Sahara	3.6	−6	Strong for decrease in DJF and MAM
Southern Europe and Mediterranean	3.5	−12	Strong for decrease in all seasons

Source: Christensen and Hewitson (2007)
Note: J, F, M, A, M, J, J, A, S, O, N and D refer to the months of the year

include a range of voluntary carbon markets as well as a growing range of other initiatives, such as the UNDP green funds.

Modelling and measuring climate change

Most assessments of future climate change are based on the results of models that rely on a range of data and scenarios. The diversity of data required and the need to maintain consistency between different scenarios pose substantial challenges to researchers, and help to account for the divergence in predictions generated. General Circulation Models are used to simulate the response of the global climate system to increasing greenhouse gas concentrations. These complex models represent the physical processes found in the atmosphere, ocean and land surface. Predicting climate change for many African regions is particularly complex, because of the limited data available from the past and present, and poor understanding of how changes in the characteristics of land, sea and atmosphere interact. All models show that Africa will warm during this century, with the drier subtropical regions warming more than the moister tropics. According to the IPCC, annual rainfall is likely to decrease in much of Mediterranean Africa and the northern Sahara, with the decline being more marked towards the Mediterranean coast. Rainfall in southern Africa is also likely to decrease while an increase in average rainfall is expected in East Africa. Rainfall trends in the West African Sahel, the Guinea Coast and the southern Sahara are much less certain, with some models predicting an increase and others a decrease. Box 2.1 shows how the people of the Sahel responded to shifts in rainfall over the last thirty years.

Predicting subregional climate change in Africa

The climate of East Africa is particularly interesting owing to the combination of its proximity to the Indian Ocean circulation system, its complex topography, with the African Rift Valley and Ethiopian highlands to the north, and the existence of large lakes in the region. Predictions of climate change over the twenty-first century from General Circulation Models suggest an increase of more than 10–20 per cent in rainfall overall, but a shift in its distribution, with an increase from December to February and a fall from June to August. Air temperatures are expected to increase in a range between 1.5°C and 5.8°C to 2080, depending on the region. There is considerable uncertainty regarding these predictions, however, and what they mean for particular districts within the larger subregion. Without greater investment in collecting and analysing climate data from different parts of Africa, it will be impossible to refine and test the models currently available.

Translating changes in climate to impacts on the ground

The impacts of climate change on Africa include increased aridity, sea level rise, reduced fresh water availability, cyclones, coastal erosion, deforestation, loss of forest quality, woodland degradation, coral bleaching, the spread of malaria and impacts on food security. Although there remains work to be done in the fine-tuning of models and their results, the scale of the problems that lie ahead necessitates increased investment in building more resilient systems, whether for urban centres, agriculture, energy generation or water supply. Building resilience in agricultural, forestry, urban and water sectors is discussed within each of the forthcoming chapters.

Development and climate change

In 2000, the UN member states signed up to the Millennium Development Goals (MDGs) as symbolizing the global aspirations for development, especially for poor nations. A review of progress in 2005 showed that these goals were still out of reach for many African nations. Adding climate change on top of existing development pressures is likely to damage economic growth and well-being even further.

Achieving Goal 1, which calls for the eradication of extreme poverty and hunger, will be hindered by changes in rainfall patterns that threaten crop production and food security, so contributing to increased hunger and loss of income. Any increase in extreme weather events such as flooding will cause displacement of communities and destroy infrastructure, which might block access to

Box 2.1   Climate vulnerability in the Sahel

The Sahel region lies along the southern edge of the Sahara desert, extending nearly five thousand kilometres from Cape Verde and Senegal in the west, through Mali, Niger and Chad to Sudan and the Horn of Africa in the east. It is a transitional zone between the arid Sahara and the savannahs and tropical forest that border the coast. The Sahel has always been exposed to a variable climate. Farming in this region relies on three to four months of summer rainfall, followed by a long dry season, but with average rainfall of between 200 and 600 mm, the variation from year to year can reach 30 per cent or more. Irrigated agriculture is limited to a few major schemes, such as the Office du Niger in Mali, and along the banks of major rivers, lakes and other seasonal watercourses.

The Sahel suffered severe droughts in the early 1970s and 1980s, causing major losses of harvests and livestock, and associated humanitarian crises. While Niger experienced another bad famine in 2005, other parts of the region have been spared further droughts and famine on the scale of the 1970s and 1980s.

Climate models generate mixed predictions for the future Sahelian climate. Some maintain that the Sahel region will be even drier in the twenty-first century, owing to hotter temperatures and higher levels of evaporation. Whatever rain does fall will therefore evaporate at a faster rate, exacerbating the already arid conditions. Others have a more optimistic view of likely rainfall trends, such that agricultural conditions might improve at least for the next twenty to thirty years.

schools, so hindering universal primary education, which is Goal 2. The impacts of climate change on agricultural productivity or access to water will place additional burdens on women in terms of labour and health, reducing time for income-generating activities, leading to a worsening of women's empowerment and gender equality, the target of Goal 3. Reducing child mortality, improving maternal health and combating disease, which are Goals 4, 5 and 6, will be impacted directly by changes in water availability and indirectly by shifts in the distribution of disease, displacement of people and damage to infrastructure by extreme events. Lack of achievement with these latter goals, along with loss of biodiversity and greater stress on natural ecosystems, will make it even harder to achieve Goal 7, that of environmental stability. The collective response needed to tackle global climate calls for the formation of global partnerships, which is the focus of Goal 8.

Preparing for climate change – adaptation and building resilience

Climate change has implications for many sectors. Response measures are needed at all levels, from local to international, by a diversity of actors both inside and outside government. Some measures involve being prepared to cope with the impacts, such as disaster preparedness. Others concern ways to build greater resilience into environmental, economic, social and institutional systems. Resilience refers to the ability of a region, country, city, village or household to protect itself from adverse impacts and recover from damage.

Adaptation planning at regional level is especially important for trans-boundary water management, which is discussed in Chapter 3. Regional planning, such as the African Union's ClimDev[5] programme, will be essential, and action above the country level is needed for design of some disaster risk reduction activities, such as regional food purchases, and other forms of regional risk pooling (Jallow and Downing 2007). Other cross-sectoral measures include research and technology development on common problems, as well as observation and communication systems. For example, the Sahara and Sahel Observatory system supports thirty monitoring centres across the northern half of Africa that provide environmental surveillance information and early warning systems, and help with management of water and drought preparedness.

At national level, governments can use a range of policies to help people adapt to climate change. Adaptation in the water sector is particularly critical. Having experienced one-third of all water-related disasters worldwide over the past ten years, Africa urgently needs better management of water resources at all levels, including better management of major rivers, investment in irrigation and water-harvesting techniques, increased water storage at local level, and improved water access for domestic purposes.

Climate risks need to be integrated into national development plans and strategies. But owing to the interconnectedness of the sectors affected by climate change, national governments in Africa and elsewhere have struggled to know where and how to start. Although Poverty Reduction Strategy Papers (PRSPs) outline each government's principal objectives and budgetary allocations, few mention climate change.

Calculating the costs of adaptation is highly speculative, whether in Africa or elsewhere. Stern (2006) states that 'adaptation is so broad and cross-cutting – affecting economic, social and environmental conditions and vice versa – that it is difficult to attribute costs clearly'. Adaptation should be undertaken at many levels at the same time, including at the household and community level, and many of these initiatives will be self-funded. Building on estimates from the World Bank, Stern and the IPCC, Oxfam estimates that adaptation in developing countries will cost at least US$50–80 billion each year (Oxfam 2007). Currently, there are a series of adaptation funding sources available, but most of these have total funds of under $100 million. Such sums are tiny in relation to the scale of the challenges to be faced at country and continent level. Hence, additional resources are urgently required to start to put in place an effective programme of adaptation.

The thirteenth Conference of the Parties at Bali in December 2007 set up an adaptation fund (AF), under the authority of the UNFCCC. The adaptation fund will get the proceeds from a 2 per cent levy on transactions under the CDM. There are proposals to top this up with a tax on airline flights, sea-freight bunker fuel, a Tobin tax on foreign-exchange flows, or a levy on the auctioning of emission rights. The Least Developed Countries (LDCs) and small island states argue, rightly, that this is not aid but compensation for the damage caused to them by those responsible for emissions. So, rather than have to follow the cumbersome procedures laid down by aid agencies and development banks, the funds should be made available in much simpler ways, with a minimum of red tape.

National Adaptation Programmes/Plans of Action (NAPAs)

At the 2001 meeting of the UNFCCC, it was agreed that all LDCs, the majority of which are in Africa, would receive support to identify their most urgent adaptation needs through the preparation of NAPAs, and many of these have now been prepared (see Box 2.2). The NAPA process is criticized by some, however, as being inadequately financed, biased towards small-scale projects, and

---

Box 2.2 Burkina Faso's National Adaptation Plan of Action

Under the UNFCCC each LDC has agreed to prepare a NAPA in which it identifies priority activities to help it adapt to climate change. The 2007 NAPA for Burkina Faso identified four sectors as particularly vulnerable to climate change: water supply, agriculture, livestock and forestry/fisheries. These four sectors form the foundation of the Burkinabé economy and are vulnerable to four aspects of climate change: decline and variability in rainfall, flooding, rising temperatures and increased wind speeds.

1 Water supply – a projected increase in the frequency of heavy rains and flooding is expected to lead to greater erosion and siltation within each of Burkina's four major river basins. When combined with projected decreases in overall rainfall, the NAPA authors anticipate this will result in reduced run-off by 2050, ranging from 30 per cent for the Nakanbé basin to 73 per cent for the Mouhoun basin. Given the enormous reliance of the population on these rivers for

---

with weak links into broader human development goals. While NAPA documents identify a list of priority projects, they do not contain full project proposals that would allow access to funding from the Global Environment Facility (GEF) or other agencies. This is problematic, given the priority for LDCs now to address the urgent needs identified in the NAPAs.

It is widely agreed that investment in disaster preparedness produces high returns, with US$1 in costs invested in preparation yielding $7 in reduced damage. Any delay in implementation of adaptation plans will increase vulnerability and lead to significant cost increases at a later stage. Improved disaster early warning systems should also reduce vulnerability. Building on experience from 2000, the government of Mozambique has worked with donors, undertaken flood analysis, set up a new network of meteorological

domestic and irrigated water resources, the potential losses look very serious.

2 Agriculture – Burkina's NAPA predicts that average annual rainfall will drop by 3.4 per cent by 2025 and 7.3 per cent by 2050. For an economy heavily dependent on rain-fed agriculture, such a drop will have significant implications for crops across the country. For example, cotton, maize and yams have already seen harvests fall in the south as a result of drought.

3 Livestock – an expected further average rise in temperature of 1.7°C by mid-century will combine with decreased rainfall to reduce the watering points open to livestock keepers. Floods are expected to compound these threats by killing livestock.

4 Forestry/fisheries – increased erosion and siltation are expected to damage land and water ecosystems, while clearing of new land is expected to continue apace. Forestry biomass is predicted to decrease from 200 million square metres in 1999 to little more than 110 million square metres by 2050.

stations, established radio-based early warning systems and ensured mass evacuation of people from those areas most at risk. As a consequence, the timely response to the floods of early 2007 led to far fewer casualties.

Adaptation at the local level is essential to build resilience into ecological, social and institutional systems on the ground (Thornton et al. 2006). Strengthening local, indigenous coping strategies and building on community institutions are key ways forward. Over generations, many African societies have developed ways of coping with drought and other climate shocks, such as diversifying their crops and animals, sending family members off on migration, and moving to higher rainfall areas. They also have systems for gathering and interpreting information on the weather and adapting their farming practices accordingly. In some countries, the meteorological department has been working with farmers to train them in basic data collection, and to plan a farming calendar based on weather forecasts, which also helps highlight risks of certain crop disease outbreaks, such as mildew. Working together with climate scientists has helped farmers increase their yields of millet, sorghum and maize in areas covered by such schemes.

Migration as a response to floods and droughts is a well-known means of reacting to climatic stress. For example, communities in some disaster-prone areas have moved to upland areas either with support from government or on their own, using networks and contacts to help them. As noted earlier, however, large flows of migrants can generate serious problems in their destinations, given scarce land, water and shelter, from which conflict can develop.

Conclusion

The predictions from scientists show that Africa will face serious challenges given the expected climate change impacts. Temperatures are expected to increase across the continent, which will lead to increased plant stress and increased risks of drought. Rainfall is expected to decline significantly in southern Africa, and the North African region, including the Sahara desert. East Africa is expected to become wetter, with rain falling in more intense storms, causing greater risks of flooding. The models show mixed results for what is likely to happen to West Africa's rainfall. These shifts in rainfall will bring major impacts on the ground, in terms of crop yields, water availability, disease incidence and flood damage. Effective adaptation to the changes under way and building resilient livelihood systems will be key in helping prevent serious losses to people's incomes and assets. National Adaptation Programmes of Action are one response to these challenges, now seeking funding support. The sums currently made available through international mechanisms are tiny in comparison with the scale of need. New predictable sources of funding will be needed, such as through an airline tax, or allocation of revenues from auctioning carbon allowances. But money alone will not be enough. Rather, we need to redesign development plans to emphasize resilience rather than maximum yield, and reduce vulnerability through greater attention to the needs of the poorest.

Global climate change and Africa

3 | Water

Introduction

Water is at the heart of human existence, and where it is plentiful, people and ecosystems can flourish. Global warming has major impacts on the global water cycle and, hence, on rainfall, soil moisture, rivers and sea level. This chapter describes how water availability is likely to change in different regions of Africa, with some areas suffering major shortfalls while others risk increased floods. Water not only provides for household and cropping needs, but also provides a significant source of energy through hydropower schemes. The African continent hosts a large number of river basins shared by several states, where management of the river needs to accommodate the changing interests of each country, while responding to shifts in rainfall and water availability. Overall sub-Saharan Africa has significant water resources for household, agricultural and energy needs, but needs much more investment. The challenge of climate change should prompt further progress in improving access to clean water, given its huge value in maternal and child health, as well as spurring economic growth.

Water and development

When communities gain access to safe drinking water, the positive changes this brings are wide ranging and remarkable, as shown in Box 3.1. Water is also of great importance to the economies of many African nations, which depend on it directly for agricultural production and industry, and indirectly as a valuable source of hydropower. Such dependence on water was made evident during the 1991/92 drought, which led to an 8–9 per cent reduction in Malawi's GDP (Stern 2006), and during the drought of 1999/2000, leading to a fall of 16 per cent in Kenya's GDP.

When water is scarce, more creativity is needed to design the technology and institutions essential to make life possible in harsh conditions. Many ancient civilizations built up successful systems for managing scarce water resources, along with the rules and responsibilities that made prosperity possible. The decline and collapse of kingdoms and empires have often been attributed to a failure to maintain water systems, or to changes in rainfall, which meant people were no longer able to cope (Diamond 2005).

The IPCC (2007) describes how global warming will bring about major shifts in water availability through its impact on the global water cycle and associated weather systems. As noted by the Stern Review of 2006, 'People will feel the impact of climate change most strongly through changes in the distribution of water around the world and its seasonal and annual variability' (Stern 2006). As the temperature rises, the water-holding capacity of the air increases exponentially. This means that global warming will bring about an atmosphere more heavily laden with moisture, which will intensify

Water

33

the force of the water cycle, and lead to more severe floods and droughts. Higher temperatures generate more energy to drive storms and hurricanes, leading to bigger, more powerful extreme events (ibid.). Higher temperatures also increase the amount of water that evaporates from rivers, lakes and ponds, as well as increasing the speed at which soils dry after rainfall, hence reducing the humidity, so that crops experience greater stress. According to the IPCC, by 2020 between 75 and 250 million people across as many as twenty-five African nations (Bates et al. 2008) will be at greater risk of water stress[2] as a consequence of global warming.

Rainfall and water availability

The movement and timing of the world's large weather systems combine with other factors, including mountains and landscape, to explain differences in access to fresh water across the African continent. This varied pattern stretches from the rain-abundant mountains of Lesotho and the enormous flows draining into the Congo river basin to the extensive marshlands of the Okavango Delta, the Sudd and the inner Niger Delta, and the springs and artesian wells in the deserts of North Africa.

One useful way of thinking about water availability and its impact on people is to divide it into its 'green' and 'blue' components. Green water is that fraction of rainfall which goes into the soil, generates moisture and supports plant life. It is not returned to groundwater and rivers, and eventually evaporates or is absorbed into plants. Blue water, on the other hand, represents the fraction of rainfall that runs into rivers and, as groundwater, into aquifers from which it can then be withdrawn for human use. Green water is a very important resource for global food production. About 60 per cent of the world's staple food production relies on rain-fed farming, and hence on green water. In sub-Saharan Africa, rain-fed agriculture for both food and industrial crops accounts for 95 per cent of cultivated land, with only 5 per cent under irrigation, the latter made up largely of industrial crops, such as cotton, tobacco and sugar. Comparatively lower levels of rainfall in northern Africa mean that the share of rain-fed farming in the region is much lower, and irrigation water pumped from aquifers (blue water) accounts for a greater share of crop production. Moisture stored in soil is the main water source for Africa's extensive grasslands, on which livestock production relies. The green water supply is also vital for the production of wood and other forestry products.

In areas where global warming causes a decline in rainfall, there will be less green water available for plant growth and maintenance of ecosystems. Blue water flows will fall as well, with less water available in rivers, lakes and ponds, and a decrease in water available for withdrawal via wells from the water table. Where rainfall increases, the balance between the green and blue water components will shift, depending on whether it comes in big storms, or in more continuous lighter showers. Storms will generate more run-off, with less water seeping into soils, and increased levels of erosion and baring of soils. River flow may well increase but will bring with it a higher sediment load of soil. If rain comes in gentler form, a higher proportion will be absorbed by the soil and percolate into the ground, improving moisture availability for plant growth.

Farmers and land users can try to increase the green water component, by modifying soil conditions so that less rainfall runs off the land, and by building anti-erosion barriers, such as terraces, bunds and infiltration pits. Planting shelter belts to reduce wind speeds and hence levels of moisture evaporation from the land also helps to conserve the green water component, reducing stress in plants and increasing resilience in cropping systems. Farmers can try to increase their access to the blue water component by establishing ways to harvest and store water (such as the large 'tanks' or reservoirs found in much of India), and by tapping into water from rivers and deep water tables.

What do the climate models predict?

While warming is expected everywhere on earth in the decades to come, the amount predicted generally increases moving from the tropics to the poles. Rainfall is a more complex variable, but also has some latitude-dependent features. The bulk of the African continent is tropical or subtropical, and feels the marked seasonal

Box 3.2   The Intertropical Convergence Zone

The Intertropical Convergence Zone (ITCZ), also known as the monsoon trough or the doldrums, is formed near the equator by the meeting of the north-east and south-east trade winds. These winds force moist air upwards, causing water vapour to condense out as the air rises and cools. Areas directly under the ITCZ receive more than two hundred days of rainfall each year. The ITCZ follows the band on the earth where the sun's radiation is strongest and most direct, and migrates north and south through the year, as the earth tilts on its axis, relative to the sun. In Africa, the ITCZ is located just south of the Sahel, but it can shift as much as 40°–45° of latitude north or south of the equator over the course of the year. In West Africa, the start of the monsoon depends on the northward progression of the ITCZ over the period June to August, when the Sahel and the southern Sahara receive most of their rainfall. In southern Africa, the annual rainfall is greater and distributed over two rainy seasons, one in the spring and the other in the autumn. Even small shifts in the position of the ITCZ rain belts result in large local changes in rainfall, bringing severe droughts or flooding.[3]

shift of the tropical rainfall belts. One of these belts, the Inter-tropical Convergence Zone (ITCZ), spans the continent, and the timing of its movement back and forth determines seasonal rainfall and, hence, water availability for many African states, stretching from Swaziland to Liberia.

The ITCZ normally follows the predictable seasonal pattern of change in surface temperature and brings reliable rainfall. The exception to this rule occurs every three to eight years, however, when a climate phenomenon called the El Niño Southern Oscillation (ENSO) creates unusually warm sea surface temperatures in the tropical Pacific and causes a shift in movement of the ITCZ (see Box 3.3).

Box 3.3 The El Niño Southern Oscillation

The El Niño Southern Oscillation is the most prominent source of inter-annual variability in weather and climate around the world. The cause of El Niño and its opposing state, La Niña, is not fully understood. In normal years the trade winds flowing into the ITCZ push warm ocean surface water from east to west across the Pacific Ocean. This warm air then rises and cools, leading to rainfall in the western Pacific and relatively dry weather in the east. El Niño occurs when these trade winds slacken or reverse, allowing the warm ocean surface water normally residing in the western tropical Pacific to be pushed eastwards. This results in heavy rainfall over South America (east Pacific) and droughts in the western Pacific, and along the coast of east and southern Africa. In contrast, when a strong La Niña occurs, unusually warm water is piled up in the west Pacific. This leads to excessive rains in the west and drought conditions in the eastern Pacific.[4]

In Africa, the effect of El Niño often prevents the ITCZ from moving as far south as normal, especially over the eastern half of the continent. This means that areas in southern Africa, at the southernmost limit of the ITCZ's annual migration, are deprived of rain. The reduced southerly movement means that the ITCZ spends longer over the northern regions and hence these areas receive greater rainfall. In 1997/98, the ENSO created extremely wet conditions over eastern Africa and was partly to blame for the devastating floods in Mozambique. Research has shown that ENSO events and associated changes in eastern Pacific sea temperatures account for 60 per cent of the variation in annual yields of maize in Zimbabwe.

In West Africa, there are some effects on rainfall patterns from ENSO events, but these remain small owing to the greater distance involved. Though we do not know exactly how the temperature of oceans affects the larger weather system, the oceans do play

Water

an important role in affecting rainfall. The strength of the West African monsoon seems to be closely linked to warm sea surface temperatures and stronger wind speeds in the Gulf of Guinea (Paeth et al. 2005). For East Africa, sea surface temperatures in the Indian Ocean are also an important indicator for predicting drought and heavy rain conditions over the southern half of the continent.

As far as the impact of global warming on the ENSO is concerned, observations have shown that the frequency and intensity of these events have increased in recent years. Our current climate models, however, are unable accurately to reproduce the complexity of the climate system, so it is not yet proven that the greater intensity of recent ENSO events is directly linked to climate change.

Climate change and access to water

The overall predictions for changes in temperature for different regions of Africa over the next 100 years were described earlier. These showed that there was a high level of agreement on an average rise in temperature across the continent of 3.2–3.6°C, and on North Africa, southern Africa and the Sahara becoming drier. East Africa is expected to become wetter, but the evidence for changes to rainfall in West Africa is much less certain. Clearly these estimates are at a very macro scale and mask a range of more complex interactions and local differences. But they demonstrate the likelihood of major problems of water stress in northern and southern Africa. Taking the Ouergha watershed in Morocco as an example, Agoumi (2003) shows that a 1°C increase in temperature could reduce run-off by 10 per cent, assuming that rainfall levels remain the same.

It is not only the amount of water available which is important, but also being able to predict changes in its availability. In recent times, there has been considerable volatility in lake levels, owing to periods of intense drought followed by extreme rainfall events. For example, Lake Victoria rose by 1.7 metres and Lake Tanganyika rose by 2.1 metres during the year following the 1997 flood. Too much water, like too little water, plays havoc with municipal planning and service provision, such as hydroelectricity production and water

Box 3.4 Flooding in Mozambique

In early 2000, Mozambique, one of the world's poorest countries, suffered the worst flooding in half a century with floodwaters rising to 8 metres (more than 26 feet) and submerging many areas of the capital, Maputo. Over 45,000 people were rescued from rooftops, trees and other isolated areas. Ninety per cent of the country's irrigation system was damaged. More than 110,000 farming families lost their crops and stock, 630 schools were closed and 42 health clinics were destroyed, including the second-largest hospital in the country. The Mozambican government requested $450 million in international aid to help to rebuild the country's roads, bridges and power supplies.

In late December 2006, southern Africa, including Mozambique, experienced more severe flooding, and two months later, on 22 February, tropical Cyclone Favio made landfall in Mozambique's central province, by coincidence landing on the same date as the devastating cyclone in 2000. Thanks to considerable investment in disaster preparedness, however, the damage wrought in 2006/07 was much less severe than it had been six years earlier.

treatment, as well as causing localized flooding, contaminating wells and depositing debris that blocks drainage channels.

Box 3.4 describes the consequences of too much rain in southern Africa and the floods in Mozambique, providing a powerful reminder that, while people complain that water is often in short supply, too much water at the wrong time of year can be as damaging as too little.

Why is water scarce in Africa?

Even if rainfall levels remained stable, there is the potential for water scarcity to occur as a consequence of many other factors, such as increased needs of growing populations, and the demands

Water

39

of economic growth. A comparison of access to water and levels of water stress, in different regions of the world, reveals some startling differences. Water stress is most evident in northern Africa, where it is estimated that up to 240 million people are exposed to water stress, and countries such as Egypt and Libya are currently extracting more than 90 per cent of the water available to them each year. In Tunisia, Algeria, Morocco and Sudan this figure is greater than 50 per cent. With a likely decline in rainfall plus higher temperatures and therefore increased evaporation, there is a high likelihood of greater water stress across all sectors, from agriculture and domestic use to industry. For Egypt, where irrigated agriculture provides 20 per cent of GDP and uses 90 per cent of the country's water, finding a way to manage water use in a sustainable manner is an ever stronger imperative.[5] Sub-Saharan Africa also has problems with water stress, with an estimated 140 million people affected, despite it using only 2 per cent of its potential water supply. Part of the cause of the mismatch between availability and need is the very limited investment to date in water infrastructure, at micro- and macro-levels.

More effective use of available water

Investment in micro-level water supplies, such as small dams, wells, boreholes and micro-irrigation, can be very valuable for domestic and small-scale farming purposes. Small dams have allowed market gardens to emerge out of the desert, bringing much-needed cash and extra foodstuffs. Throughout the dry Sahel, small-scale irrigation offers a valuable addition to incomes, especially in the dry season. Take, for example, the small onion gardens of the Dogon plateau in Mali, which are constructed on slabs of rock next to a good water source, with earth brought from elsewhere (Reij et al. 1996). Similar constructions to raise a harvest of tobacco, tomatoes and fruit trees are found in many other dry areas.

Another approach involves a combination of investment in technology with a rethink of the tenure and incentive systems surrounding access to water and land, and the security of rights. For example, in the case of the large irrigated scheme known as the Office du Niger in central Mali, since the early 1990s a major programme to rehabilitate the canals and water management system has been accompanied by giving farmers stronger rights to the land they farm and providing an incentive for them to improve the quality of their plots. This has led to a doubling in yields, a second harvest and a boost to household incomes, due to better use of irrigation water. Equally, encouraging traditional methods of rainwater harvesting can greatly improve crop resilience at micro-level, as described in Chapter 4.

Water pricing can also help provide incentives for better management of scarce water supplies, and help shift water away from low-value irrigated crops to those that earn higher revenue. But a policy of water pricing needs to recognize poor people's limited ability to pay. In the case of South Africa, basic needs always receive priority in water allocations, followed by strategic uses, such as power generation and key industries. In general, water for irrigation is the first to be restricted when supplies run low.[6]

Water storage

Large dams help store water for public use and irrigation, even in years of low rainfall, as well as moderating flooding, when rainfall is abundant. The importance of providing greater water storage is made evident in a report that found that better water storage could have prevented a 16 per cent decline in Kenya's gross domestic product (GDP) attributed to the 1999/2000 drought. Africa does, however, host some 1,272 large dams, with one of the largest being the Cahora Bassa dam in Mozambique, which holds 55.8 square kilometres of water. Of these large dams, 19 per cent are for multipurpose use, with the remaining 81 per cent being for a single purpose. Of the latter, 66 per cent are for irrigation, 25 per cent for public water supply, and the remainder are for other purposes, including power generation (WCD 2000). Although this number of dams sounds impressive, there are huge disparities in their distribution across the continent, with nearly half in South Africa alone, whereas Tanzania, a country with nearly the same landmass and population, has only two large dams. Small dams are

41

of greater potential importance in many parts of Africa, particularly for storage of domestic and livestock water supplies, and generate fewer problems than large-scale dams, which usually involve the displacement and resettlement of populations.

Water for energy

Stored water is also used to generate hydropower. Access to electricity is a good indicator of a country's overall socio-economic development. Access opens up and multiplies a number of benefits for urban and rural people, from providing lights that enable schoolchildren to do their homework at night, to generating power for small businesses. As stated by the World Bank's energy director, Jamal Saghir, 'Every one percent increase in the rate of electrification yields a one percent drop in poverty.' For many Africans, access to electricity remains beyond their reach, with only 53 per cent of urban and 8 per cent of rural sub-Saharan Africa being connected to a supply. In northern Africa, the figures are considerably better, with 99 per cent and 88 per cent respectively of urban and rural populations being serviced (IEA 2004). Where there is access to electricity, particularly in sub-Saharan Africa, much of it is generated from hydroelectric plants. Figure 3.1 shows the percentage contribution of hydroelectric power to electricity supplies, which ranges from almost total reliance in Mozambique, Ethiopia and the Democratic Republic of Congo to less than 2 per cent of electricity demand in South Africa. Investing more in hydropower would help to diversify the energy mix needed to meet South Africa's growing demand for electricity, while at the same time reducing its greenhouse gas emissions. Other new sources of power of significance for rural areas some distance from the grid include solar panels, biogas and various forms of biofuel.

Hydropower in Africa has considerable unexploited potential, and many new projects are planned or under construction. The main regions being considered are the Congo river, the Nile river and the Zambezi river. Given the social and environmental concerns of such projects, however, there also needs to be a shift in policy from reliance on investment in large dams towards encouraging

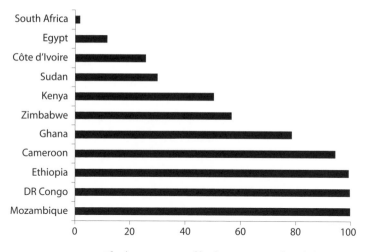

FIGURE 3.1 The importance of hydropower to electricity generation in Africa (%) (*source*: IEA)

a more diverse range of micro-generation options (WCD 2000). In Uganda, for example, estimates suggest that there is good 'mini-hydro' potential on seventy-one rivers but currently only six small hydropower plants are in operation. Equally, small-scale hydropower in Madagascar has shown good potential for meeting the needs of small businesses and medium-sized towns.

Hydropower and climate change

Estimating future returns from investment in hydropower is complicated by the potential impacts of climate change. One element concerns the loss of water by evaporation from the reservoir surface, which is estimated on average at 1.1 metres of depth per year. This can be much greater in higher temperatures, with loss from evaporation behind the Aswan High Dam on the Nile river estimated to be 2.7 metres of depth, which constitutes 11 per cent of the reservoir capacity. The projected temperature increase for Africa of between 3.2 and 3.6°C by 2080, combined with other meteorological conditions, such as higher wind speed, will further increase rates of evaporation, though less so in areas of high humidity.

Lower levels of rainfall will lead to a reduction in run-off and consequent loss of water storage in dams, as was seen in the case of Kenya in 2000. Drought had a major impact on Kenya's power supply, causing a deficit in power generation of 400 megawatts. To minimize damage to the economy, estimated as $660 million over six months, from power rationing, Kenya requested a loan of $72 million from the World Bank to lease diesel generators to make up some of the shortfall. Other impacts of climate change include flooding, caused by an increased intensity of rainfall, which has the potential to discharge large amounts of soil and debris into reservoirs, causing damage and blocking up the system. Sparse vegetation and the desiccation of soils during the dry season combined with the high intensity of storms when rainfall does arrive make soils particularly vulnerable to erosion. The resulting siltation of dams causes problems for the operation of the turbines, as well as shortening the operational life of the dam.

Sharing water

The African continent hosts over eighty shared river basins, covering about 60 per cent of the continent's area. While some are relatively minor in area and flow, involving no more than two neighbouring states, thirteen others are major basins of enormous size and significance, such as the Nile, Niger and Zambezi, each of which touches the geographic area of ten or more nations. Each of these river basins contains a unique hydrological system with its own mosaic of land and water use. This means that the impact of climate change will be different from one catchment to the next and will require a management system to match. International rivers in Africa pose particular challenges because of competing national interests and few well-established mechanisms for cooperative action between nations that share the major river basins.

Niger river basin

The Niger river, with a total length of 4,100 kilometres, is the third-longest river in Africa, after the Nile and the Congo, and the longest and largest river in West Africa.[7] Its basin spreads over

> ## Box 3.5 *Traditional water use rights*
>
> Traditional rights to water in the Sahel remain strong. They determine when and for how long people can have access to water for livestock and other purposes. Access to water points in arid areas is essential for herds to use neighbouring grazing lands. People or institutions that govern the right to water can therefore determine access to adjacent land. This power helps in limiting the number of grazing animals and minimizing environmental damage around watering points. Lack of clear rights can also act as a trigger for conflict between competing groups seeking water for their herds.
>
> In eastern Niger, for example, the government installed a network of water points aimed at improving conditions for herding groups. Because these points are publicly owned, however, there are no traditional rights associated with them. An increasing number of herds have converged on the area and there have been a series of violent clashes between those groups with long-term rights in the area and newcomers seeking fresh water and pastures.
>
> Adapting to climate change will require clearer recognition of rights to control water and land access in dry areas (Cotula 2006).

ten countries, including Guinea, Mali, Burkina Faso, Benin, Niger, Chad, Cameroon and Nigeria. The river is critically important for Mali, Niger and Nigeria, with the first two countries almost entirely dependent on it for their water resources, generating power, supplying cities and irrigating agriculture, as well as for river transport from the trade in goods. The country of Niger, in particular, is placed in a complex geographic and diplomatic situation, with nearly 90 per cent of its total water originating outside its borders, coming from the Niger river and other tributaries from neighbouring Burkina Faso and Benin.

Water

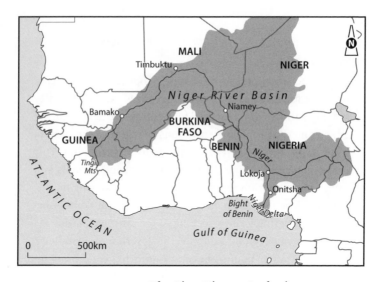

FIGURE 3.2 The River Niger water basin

The quantity of water entering Mali from Guinea (40 km³/yr) is greater than the quantity of water entering Nigeria from Niger (36 km³/yr), some 1,800 kilometres farther downstream. This enormous reduction in river flow is due to three factors: the hydropower scheme at Selingué, the Canal du Sahel, leading water northwards to the rice fields of the Office du Niger, and high levels of seepage and evaporation in the inner Niger delta. Equally, there is very little water flowing into the river from the northern left bank over its course through Mali and Niger.[8] There are numerous plans for increased use of the River Niger's waters to satisfy rising demand from cities and industries, such as a series of dams and extension of irrigated areas.

Anticipating the need to manage water flows and projects within the Niger catchment led, in 1980, to the establishment of the Autorité du Bassin du Niger (ABN) or Niger Basin Authority. Although, to date, this agency has been largely ineffective, it is now being revitalized, and its future success will be imperative, especially in the light of potential challenges posed by climate change within the Niger river basin. As with the Nile basin, more work is needed to promote international and basin-level collaboration, to collect data on climate and hydrology, and adopt water management approaches that recognize the multiple demands on this trans-boundary resource. Given that the coming decades will see increasing competition for water in many places, institutions capable of addressing allocation and efficiency in ways that minimize risks of conflict will be urgently needed.

Water wars?

The risk of increased water scarcity has stimulated a large and growing body of literature warning of future 'water wars'. Examples commonly quoted include the potential for conflict over the Nile waters, with growing needs for irrigation water in Ethiopia, Sudan and Egypt. In reality, conflict over water has been rare to date. In modern times, only seven minor skirmishes have been waged over international waters; invariably other interrelated issues are more important factors. Conversely, over 3,600 treaties have been signed over different aspects of international waters, 145 since 2000, many of which show great creativity in dealing with this critical resource (Barnaby 2009). This is not to say that armed conflict has not taken place over water, only that such disputes are generally at a very local level, involving competing herdsmen, or water-use sectors. See Box 3.6 for a case study from Ghana.

In recognition of the central importance of water for human life, Priscoli (1998) describes water as 'humanity's great learning ground for building community'. Shared interests along a waterway usually trump the potential for conflict and, once water management institutions are in place, they tend to be resilient. The more valuable lesson from managing international waters is that it can provide strong grounds for cooperation, inciting violence only as the exception, rather than the rule.

Successful trans-boundary water laws have historically been multilateral and focus both on joint management and on how best to develop these resources, for the benefit of all riparian nations. Such agreements govern Lake Chad, the Niger, Senegal and Volta basins, and the Okavango delta, and include most or all riparian

Water

*Box 3.6   The challenges of sharing water within a single
country – the case of Ghana*

The Volta dam was constructed in 1965 as a means to generate hydropower for the capital, Accra, and for the bauxite
smelting process, seen by Nkrumah – Ghana's first president
– as key to Ghana's industrial development. But while the
electricity and jobs provided by the dam benefit the south
of the country, the waters of the White and Black Volta stem
from the north of Ghana, where incomes and economic
opportunities are much lower. A recent government report
estimates that demand for irrigation could increase in the
north twelvefold by 2050, as a result of climate change and
population increase. Managing the trade-off between providing electricity for urban growth and water for farmers'
needs is critical for bridging the high levels of regional inequality and avoiding conflict (Brown and Crawford 2008).

states, with the intention of promoting economic development
through investment to reduce water scarcity.

Managing water resources for the future

Improving access to water and sanitation is crucial to spurring growth and sustaining economic development in Africa. The
Millennium Declaration of 2000 identified access to safe water as
a key factor within several of the Millennium Development Goals
(MDGs), which world leaders have pledged to achieve by 2015.
Access to safe water can, for example, lead to a reduction in poverty
levels; it can raise school attendance and reduce maternal and child
mortality rates. Progress in improving access to drinking water in
sub-Saharan Africa has been reasonably impressive, with coverage
increasing from 49 to 58 per cent between 1990 and 2002. If the
MDG 7 target of 75 per cent coverage by 2015 is to be reached,
however, then faster progress needs to be made (WHO/UNICEF
2008). The extra challenge in attaining these MDG goals within the

context of climate change, with its potential to bring variations in rainfall and extreme weather events, is likely to place additional strains on poorer African nations.

Conclusion

This chapter has shown the importance of water for people, crops, livestock and energy generation. Changes in the availability of water and timing of rainfall are major consequences from global warming, and will have significant impacts on many aspects of life for rural and urban dwellers across the African continent. There are many opportunities for improved water management, so that better use is made of whatever rain does fall, through soil conservation structures, micro-catchments and small dams. Equally, more attention could usefully be focused on investment in water infrastructure combined with systems for maintenance that ensure water continues to flow (Skinner 2009). It will become increasingly urgent to agree ways to plan and manage large shared river basins, so that the multiple demands on this resource are handled fairly. Water is such a vital element in daily life that it needs to be at the centre of plans for adapting to climate change.

Water

4 | Food

Introduction

Agriculture has been the backbone to the economy of most African countries, employing a large share of the population and generating incomes, tax revenues and exports. Food systems are highly diverse across the continent but they share in common a number of constraints that have kept both yields and farm incomes low. This chapter reviews some of the underlying challenges facing farmers, such as growing pressures on land, limited access to inputs and markets, and poor support from government to the smallholder sector. Global warming will bring additional multiple impacts for farming, livestock, fisheries and wild foods. Farmers will need to find ways to build more resilient systems able to adapt to changing environmental conditions, as well as taking advantage of new market opportunities. Land use patterns also have an impact on climate change through release or absorption of carbon into soils and vegetation. Given Africa's large land area, there may be a range of options for land-users to offer the environmental services provided by their land in exchange for finance from carbon markets.

Background

Some 70 per cent of Africans live in rural areas and depend on agriculture for a significant part of their income. In sub-Saharan Africa, agriculture accounts for 17 per cent of GDP, and 11 per cent of export earnings of the region.[1] Nevertheless, there is great variation among countries. In oil-producing Nigeria, agricultural exports account for only 0.3 per cent of export earnings, and for Mozambique 17 per cent, while the figure is over 80 per cent for Benin, Burkina Faso, Ethiopia, Malawi and Sierra Leone (World Bank 2008). Some countries rely on certain crops to make up the bulk of these exports, with Uganda, for example, depending on coffee to provide up to 55 per cent of its export earnings. As a whole, food production on the African continent has not kept pace with population growth and the shift to cities. It is reckoned that 25 per cent of food needs are provided by imports.

The last five years have witnessed extraordinary volatility in the price of food and other agricultural commodities. These price changes have brought increased revenues from sales of export crops in world markets, followed by a slump, and also difficulties for those reliant on buying food. The large increase in cereal prices in 2007 and 2008 led to riots in many African cities. In less than a year, to mid-2008, the price of wheat rose by 130 per cent and rice by 74 per cent. In Egypt, Côte d'Ivoire, Mauritania, Mozambique, Senegal and Cameroon, desperate people took to the streets to protest against the price rises. And while global food prices have dropped substantially since mid-2008, domestic prices remain high in many countries, despite reasonable harvests.

There are a number of factors responsible for the large price increases of 2007/08, which include drought in Australia and other major food-producing nations, booming demand for biofuels, which has led to a significant shift in the US maize crop to ethanol, and the impact of global speculation in commodity markets. The collapse in global markets for food and other commodities since September 2008 further demonstrates the highly integrated nature of the global economy, with the financial crisis and subsequent economic recession in the USA and Europe spilling over into all sectors and regions of the world. Whatever the causes of the 2007/08 food price hike, climate change will bring new and often harsher growing conditions for crops and livestock across the continent. While African farmers have been remarkable in their capacity to adapt to climatic uncertainty in the past, future changes will greatly test such ability to cope with change.

Food systems in Africa

The African continent hosts a very wide range of food production systems, from the tef farmers of highland Ethiopia to yam

*Box 4.1 Smallholder farming in Mali – a complex,
diverse livelihood*

Ganiba Dembele heads a family of thirty people, a middle-
sized household, in the village of Kala, central Mali. One of
three brothers living and working together, he has managed
to build up two plough teams, and a small herd of sheep and
goats. In most years, the household grows enough millet to
feed all its members through the year, but in bad years they
rely heavily on the remittances sent home by the two younger
brothers, who spend months away in the dry season. Their
activities include digging wells, weaving and the lucrative
profession of fortune-telling. They are also able to borrow
money from a relative who has invested in setting up a shop
in a nearby town, which sells a range of goods, from batteries,
cigarettes, kola nut and sweets, to kerosene, shoes, cloth and
buckets. Both women and men farm the family's land. They
cultivate short-cycle millet on several small plots of land
around the village, which receive animal dung from their
herd, and a larger field 8 kilometres away in the bush where a
longer-cycle millet is grown. This bush field is fallowed after
a few years of farming and new land is cleared. A few rows
of sesame, hibiscus and cowpea are grown, while the women
of the family are allowed time off on Mondays to tend their
own small plots of groundnuts, okra and tomatoes.

cultivators in southern Nigeria, from the irrigated rice fields in
central Mali to the large commercial cereal farms of South Africa,
and from the maize and bean smallholdings in central Kenya to
the dairy farms of Zimbabwe. The quantity and type of production are hugely variable, as a result of culture, climate and land
use patterns. For instance, Uganda produces around fifteen times
more fruit and vegetable per person (380 kilograms) than Burkina
Faso (because the national dish in Uganda is the matoke banana),
but Burkina Faso grows three times more cereal per person (263

kilograms). There are also huge regional differences in agricultural resources and production. In Algeria and Egypt, for example, over 93 per cent of the arable land is irrigated, compared with Uganda or Mozambique, where crops are mainly rain fed and less than 3 per cent of land is under irrigation (FAO 2005/06).

Livestock is also central to many African farming systems, accounting for around 30 per cent of the value of agricultural production, and providing income to 200 million people across Africa from the sale of meat, milk and other products, as well as fertilizer from dung, draught power for ploughing and transport, and providing mobile 'savings' to trade in when times are hard. Food from the farm is often supplemented with plants and game collected in the wild and with fish from lakes, rivers and the sea. Off-farm activities also add to daily income, helping people diversify the way they make a living and protect themselves from risk, as can be seen from the example of Ganiba Dembele in Mali in Box 4.1.

Trends in African agriculture

The agriculture and food sectors are subject to a large number of pressures across the continent, with demography, markets, infrastructure, investment and policy all influencing the value and productivity of the farming sector, as well as the demands being made on it. The changing pattern of climate is one further force at work, which will amplify some changes and moderate others.

Land is coming under ever greater pressure from rising population, growing urban demands, the current rush to develop land for biofuel and large-scale food production, and policies to set aside land for conservation purposes, such as national parks. Mounting competition for land, rising prices and growing tenure insecurity in many areas have prompted governments and donor agencies to review land law and administration systems, and a number of land registration programmes are now under way (Toulmin and Quan 2000; Deininger 2003; Kanji et al. 2006). In some cases, the aim is to give smallholders greater security of tenure, with the expectation that this will encourage them to invest further in their land. In others, governments are seeking to clarify which areas are

Food

available for allocation to large-scale investors, with the aim of offering such lands to incoming investors for commercial farming. Many uncertainties remain, however, given the multiple, overlapping rights and claims to land and natural resources throughout the continent and the associated risks of a land grab.

Access to inputs and markets has been a fundamental constraint on many farming systems. African farmers have had limited access to credit and inputs for raising productivity. The average use of synthetic fertilizers, for example, is 8 kilograms per hectare in Africa, in contrast to 80 kg/ha in India and more than 150 kg/ha in China (Morris et al. 2007).[2] Agricultural transport networks are poor in Africa and rapidly increasing fuel costs make it harder and more expensive for crops to reach the market. African smallholders must manage very much on their own, since they have rarely had access to the protective subsidies common in EU and US farming systems, and they lack the political clout found in many other regions.

Food imports have been growing, leading to greater dependency in many parts of the continent. African countries import, on average, 25 per cent of their food needs. Many regions have been unable to keep pace with demand from a large and rapidly urbanizing population that has increased demand for foods including rice, meat, dairy, fruit and processed cereals, such as pasta. Many of the traditional grains, such as millet and sorghum, face lower prices and levels of demand, despite being better suited to many of the continent's soils and rainfall. Underlying factors, such as drought in Ethiopia, have created chronic food shortages, while others, such as political upheaval in Zimbabwe and conflict in the Sudan, have set back agricultural production greatly.

Market opportunities are changing, with certain commodities now controlled by a very small number of buyers who can exert enormous power over the terms of trade in these goods. For example, only three companies control 45 per cent of cocoa roasting and grinding, and similar levels of concentration are found in other key commodities such as maize, cotton, soy and coffee. Changes to the retail sector have also led to big shifts in market power, with the growing strength of supermarkets in many middle- and low-income countries. For example, in South Africa the rapid growth in supermarkets has led to tighter requirements for crop quality, given the demands of their consumers. Retailers also want assured delivery of large volumes to fill their shelves, so prefer to deal with a small number of large farmers rather than face the costs of buying from many small-scale producers. Such changes mean that these new, higher-value domestic markets are difficult for smallholders to access, without extra support. In many poorer countries, the supermarket sector is much less developed, with greater reliance on local markets and traders. But there has been a rapid increase in agribusinesses supplying processed milk, meat and vegetables for urban markets and the tourism industry, as well as for export.

Agricultural science has brought few answers to African agriculture, in contrast to much of Asia. The very substantial increases in productivity and levels of investment associated with the Green Revolution elsewhere have barely touched African farmers, owing in part to the limited areas under large-scale irrigation, and consequent vulnerability of crops to rainfall fluctuations. Another factor has been the limited relevance of much crop science to the constraints faced by smallholder agriculture. There are now changes in crop research methods that are starting to bring better results, where scientists have worked closely with farmers to assess desired traits. These include disease-resistant cassava in Nigeria, improved maize hybrids in East Africa, and the NERICA rice varieties developed by the West African Rice Development Authority. The Alliance for a Green Revolution in Africa (AGRA) is investing several hundred million dollars in agricultural research to identify and spread new varieties of Africa's main staple crops. Such investments in research are critical to generating a more diverse and resistant set of seed varieties which can withstand pests and diseases, such as stem rust in wheat in Kenya and Ethiopia, as well as identifying new strains better able to survive in hotter, drier conditions. But such research needs to be firmly linked to networks of farmers – women and men – able to debate how research can best address their particular

Food

55

constraints. Research on crop breeding also needs a parallel focus on ways to improve management of water, soils, biodiversity and the functioning of the ecological systems that underlie and support crop and livestock production.

Poor storage technology and high losses from pests eat into the harvest and encourage farmers to sell their produce quickly to avoid further losses. In years of good harvest, local cereal markets are often swamped when the crop is brought in and prices fall to very low levels, only to increase by a factor of two or three later in the year, when food is in short supply.

Agricultural policies have often ignored the potential of the African smallholder sector, in favour of support to large agribusinesses, often because these have been the projects of powerful political allies of those in government (Toulmin and Gueye 2003; Belières et al. 2002). 'Modernization' of agriculture is frequently said to be needed, and necessarily involving a transformation of the sector from its reliance on family farms to large-scale commercial production. The current flurry of large-scale land transactions by private companies and sovereign wealth funds, for biofuel and food production, demonstrates the power of the 'modernization' story. The contrasting evidence that small farms offer major advantages owing to their flexibility in the face of emerging risks and opportunities is ignored, despite the advantages they offer in coping with and adapting to change.

Impacts of climate change on crop production

Temperature increase Unlike in cold regions of the world, crop production in Africa is not generally constrained by low temperatures, except in some highland areas, such as in Lesotho and Ethiopia. In fact, most crops are already being cultivated at the upper limits of their temperature range for most of the year. The overall impact of hotter temperatures on yields will depend on how this increase is distributed through the year. Where frosts are a significant constraint, such as in the Ethiopian highlands, warmer winter temperatures could bring higher yields of barley and tef. In highland Kenya, higher temperatures in winter would also be of advantage to crops, but would bring lower yields if summer temperatures rise as well. In practice, temperatures are likely to increase throughout the year, so that any gains from a warmer cool season will be balanced by losses from a hot season that becomes even hotter. Higher average temperatures add to stress on plants. In 2007, for example, Uganda's Department of Meteorology warned that just a slight increase in temperature could wipe out most of the country's coffee crop. In response, Uganda's coffee growers are implementing water and soil conservation measures to limit the impact of warmer temperatures on their crop, but serious concerns remain for the future of this crop given its central role in generating export revenue.[3]

Higher temperatures will speed up evaporation from plants and soils, so that the value of any given rainstorm is reduced. Research suggests that in North Africa, climate change could lead to a fall in yields from rain-fed agriculture of up to 50 per cent between 2000 and 2020 owing to the reduction in growing season and increased heat stress on plants (Agoumi 2003). In Egypt, for example, climate change could decrease national production of rice by 11 per cent and soybeans by 28 per cent by 2050 (Eid et al. 2006). Higher levels of CO_2 in the atmosphere should bring higher levels of plant growth, since the increased concentrations provoke greater photosynthesis. Researchers now consider, however, that for most parts of Africa this small positive effect will be more than offset by the damaging impacts of higher temperatures and water stress.

Rainfall There is some uncertainty about how rainfall patterns will change in different parts of the continent, as described earlier. In general, in northern and southern Africa, lower rainfall and increased drought are expected, while East Africa is predicted to get wetter. In West Africa, the models give quite variable results, with some predicting a 20 per cent fall and others a 20 per cent rise in rainfall levels. In practice, these general averages will pan out in very different ways on the ground, given the high levels of variability commonly experienced by many farming systems. In many dryland farming areas, for instance, it is common for one village to receive a heavy shower whereas its neighbour 10 kilometres away remains dry. This variability in rainfall is expected to continue and intensify. While the total quantity of rainfall is important, the distribution of rainfall within the growing season is also critical, since even a few days' stress beyond the plant's threshold can have significant adverse consequences on flowering, and therefore yields, particularly in fruit trees and cereals.

Extreme events Global warming is also associated with a rise in the level of moisture in the atmosphere. Every 1°C rise in temperature increases the water-holding capacity of the atmosphere by 7 per cent, causing more intensive cycling of water in the atmosphere, and increased frequency of extreme weather events. Storms, floods and unseasonably wet and cold weather can destroy crops and pasture and kill livestock, as occurred in the West African Sahel in 2001. In August and September 2007, Africa experienced its worst flooding for three decades. More than one million people were affected by flooding in twenty countries, in particular Sudan, Uganda, Ethiopia, Ghana, Togo and Burkina Faso. Heavy rains destroyed homes and crops and displaced cattle, leaving whole communities vulnerable, extremely short of food and exposed to health risks.

Sea level rise In coastal areas, sea level rise will take farmland out of production and bring risks of saltwater seepage into groundwater and coastal irrigation systems. For example, Kenya could experience loss of income from mangoes, cashew nuts and coconuts of up to $500 million owing to sea level rise by 2050 (Republic of Kenya 2007). For Egypt, sea level rise poses enormous problems, since so much of its highly productive Nile delta is less than five metres above sea level. Estimates are that a 1-metre rise in sea level will cause the inundation of about 4,500 square kilometres of farmland in the lower Nile delta, rendering Egypt even more dependent on imports of foodstuffs.

Other impacts As well as affecting plants directly, global warming and shifts in rainfall will affect distribution of pests and diseases, and the habitat of crop pollinators, such as bats, bees and moths, that are vital for successful production of fruits, vegetables and oilseeds. The recent decline in bee populations in California has shown how vital are the services provided by insects for pollinating fruit trees and a range of other crops, services that cannot easily be provided by any other means.

Livestock

Each livestock species and breed has a different capacity to deal with heat, water and nutritional stress. For example, Africa's commonest cattle breed, *Bos indicus*, increases threefold its consumption of water when the temperature rises from 10°C to 35°C (NRC 1981). Camels and goats demand far less. Changes in rainfall and temperature also affect the pattern and distribution of livestock diseases. For example, in the 1990s drought forced East African pastoralists to move their livestock to new grazing areas, thereby exposing them to greater contact with wildlife and rinderpest. Anthrax outbreaks are often associated with high temperatures and alternating heavy rainfall and drought, while Rift Valley Fever (RVF) spreads rapidly in dry areas following unusually heavy rains. The 2007 outbreak of RVF had many adverse impacts not only on animal producers but also on a large number of people involved in the livestock marketing chain. Herders suffered owing to the high level of animal deaths and abortions, as well as the loss of income from being unable to sell stock. Traders found themselves with deaths among stock and unsold animals, given the ban imposed following notification of the RVF outbreak. Slaughterhouses and butchers were also adversely affected, owing to lack of business (Wanyoike and Rich 2007). Other livestock health threats, such as tsetse fly, are closely affected by rainfall levels and associated patterns of vegetation, so that the incidence of sleeping sickness (trypanosomiasis) can be mapped fairly accurately in relation to changes in climate.

Changes in rainfall and temperature will alter the quality and

Food

59

availability of different pasture species. As rainfall declines, peren-nial grasses disappear in favour of short-cycle annual grasses which can provide good fodder, but for a briefer period, so that herds must be kept on the move. Equally, with lower rainfall, bush and tree cover thins out, so that there are fewer sources of forage in the long dry season. The impact of climate change on supplies of groundwater is less well studied, but clearly the availability of water from wells and boreholes will be critical to maintaining a viable mobile pastoral system that can make use of seasonal grazing.

Overall, however, the livestock sector is likely to be more resilient than crop production, since the mixed herds kept by smallholders are better able to cope with erratic rainfall. Transhumant systems, in which animals are moved according to seasons, are also better placed than those where animals are kept in large commercial beef and dairy farms. Cattle are more vulnerable to drought than sheep, goats and camels. In those areas likely to get hotter and drier, herd composition will change from cattle towards a greater number of small stock or camels (see Box 4.2). If this means fewer oxen can be kept, this will have a knock-on effect on capacity to plough the land. Similarly, cattle dung has been a major source of nutrients for maintaining soil fertility and crop yields, so farmers will need to find ways of 'harvesting' dung from sheep and goats instead, by kraaling them at night.

Adaptation strategies for the livestock sector include continued mobility to avoid overuse of pasture and to make best use of rainfall and pasture variability. This relies on access to pastures, often in distant areas, animal corridors to allow for the passage of stock through areas of cropping, and use of the knowledge and skills held by pastoral groups. Several governments, such as those in Mali, Guinea and Niger, have now recognized the need to reinvigorate the pastoral sector, by providing more secure rights for herders to access grazing land and water. Passage of this legislation offers hope that, after decades of neglect, the pastoral livestock economy is coming to be recognized for the value it provides to local liveli-hoods, management of grazing areas, government revenue and export earnings.

Fisheries and aquaculture

Fisheries are of great importance to food supplies, family income and employment in many parts of Africa, such as around Lakes Victoria, Malawi, Tanganyika and Chad, and along the Niger, Nile and Volta rivers. For Africa as a whole, it is reckoned that fishing provides a livelihood for nearly ten million people, a figure that has risen steadily over the last two decades. Currently, over 90 per cent of fish in Africa comes from capture, and only a small percentage from aquaculture. Fishing in coastal and fresh waters contributes over 6 per cent of GDP in Namibia and Senegal, 5 per cent in Mauritania, 4 per cent in Malawi and 3 per cent in Angola. Estimates suggest that fish provide over 50 per cent of essential protein requirements in coastal areas of countries like Ghana and Sierra Leone, and islands such as the Comoros (FAO 2006). There is, however, heavy pressure on such fisheries from industrial fleets from Europe and South-East Asia, which have bought the fishing rights from African governments seeking foreign exchange.

Food

Box 4.3 Lake Tanganyika: a valuable asset

Lake Tanganyika is the second-largest freshwater lake in the world by volume. Its 1,828-kilometre shoreline runs through Zambia, Tanzania, Democratic Republic of Congo (DRC) and Burundi, providing these countries with direct access to stocks yielding around 200,000 tons of fish per year. This source provides 25–40 per cent of the animal protein consumed in the region and supplies tens of millions of dollars in earnings for the populations of the four countries. A regional warming pattern over the last eighty years, along with a rise in surface-water temperature and decrease in wind speed, has altered aquatic systems within the lake. One example is the 20 per cent reduction in the deep-water nutrient upwelling of algae to the surface waters of the lake, where they grow. As these algae form the basis of the lake's food chain, their reduction is likely to have a negative impact on fish stocks (Jorgenson et al. 2006; FAO 1999).[4]

Climate impacts on fisheries A rise in temperature of 2°C will have an impact on the fisheries sector, but models for predicting changes here are much less advanced than for land-based systems, such as crop production. It is reckoned, however, that many of the countries likely to suffer the greatest impact will be in Africa, with Mauritania and Angola at the top of the list. To the extent that climate change will shift the distribution of fish populations, however, one region's loss may be another's gain. Impacts on African fisheries are likely to come about through several mechanisms. In coastal regions that have major lagoons or lake systems, changes in freshwater flows and a greater intrusion of salt water into lagoons will affect the species available for inland fisheries and aquaculture. Coastal fisheries dependent on sensitive ecosystems, such as coral reefs, will be hit by rising water temperatures and shifts in ocean currents. The increased frequency of extreme events will also affect the fishing industry and infrastructure. There will be more frequent loss of fishing days due to bad weather, increasing loss of nets, traps and long-lines, damage to boats and shore facilities, increased loss of life among fishermen, and increased damage to coastal communities, their houses and farmland (Allison et al. 2005).

Inland fisheries are a major source of protein and income for people hundreds of kilometres from the ocean, such as by the extensive shallow lakes found in semi-arid areas, including Lakes Chad, Kyoga and Chilwa. Analysis of rainfall variation, lake levels and fish catches indicates that there may be a significant reduction in lake and wetland area, resulting in a large fall in fish production and supply. In other areas, changes in rainfall and evaporation will have impacts on river flows and flood timing, affecting fish reproduction, growth and mortality. The resilience of these production systems depends on the existence of dry-season refuges for fish, where they can shelter to survive for several months of the dry season. A longer, hotter dry season combined with an increased number of drought years will stretch these remarkable ecosystems beyond endurance (ibid.). Conversely, if the West African region were to get wetter, this could breathe new life into the rivers and lakes on which inland fisheries depend.

Building more resilient fishery systems There are various ways to reduce the vulnerability of the fishing industry to climate change, such as reducing the fish harvest to ensure sustainable levels, strengthening management rights over water and fish stocks, and regeneration of coastal habitats to protect them from storm damage and sea level rise. There may be some positive gains to be made, such as making use of sea level rise to expand flooded areas in coastal zones where fish can be cultivated. Aquaculture, already a growing industry in DRC, Nigeria, Madagascar, South Africa, Tanzania and Uganda, among others, is a means to diversify and improve local incomes. Investment in fish breeding could help develop varieties to suit new conditions, such as warmer or more brackish waters.

Food

63

Wild foods

The consumption of food, such as fruits, nuts, tubers and game, collected from the wild remains an important way for rural households to feed themselves in a normal year, and to cope during periods of hunger or food stress. Among the maize growers of Bungoma in Kenya, people consume at least one hundred different species of vegetables and fruit drawn from the wild, while the agro-pastoral Tswana in Botswana rely on 126 plant species as sources of food (Scoones et al. 1992). In the Sahel, the *béré* shrub (*Boscia senegalensis*) offers a bitter but edible supplement to household meals during periods of shortage. Collected from the areas of bushland around the village, which are shrinking further as farmland takes over more space, these free resources from the wild are becoming few and far between. As governments parcel up 'idle' land for investors, the reserve food stocks provided by these lands for neighbouring communities are diminished and with them the resilience of local food systems.

Building a climate-resilient agricultural system

The productivity of arable land, pastures and fisheries that form Africa's food production systems will be affected both directly and indirectly by changes in climate. One forecast predicts that African countries could lose 47 per cent of their agricultural revenue by 2100 (Agoumi 2003). Others present a more optimistic projection of only 6 per cent loss. The difference between the two is the result of assumptions made about how effectively the farming sector can adapt to new conditions. Although changes brought by global warming will be significant, what is most important is whether farming communities and systems can keep pace with these changes and adapt. This depends on the resources available to them, from their own and external sources. As Dinar puts it: 'The key question is whether farmers have access to the best means of adapting to climate change in their local context.'[5]

How can farmers best be supported to adapt to climate change? African governments have consistently failed to invest much in agriculture, despite an earlier commitment to allocate at least 10 per cent of national budgets to this sector. In 2008, with global food prices at an all-time high, the UN Food and Agriculture Organization warned that 'unless the world reverses decades of neglect of small-scale farming in African and other developing countries and transforms the way food is grown, harvested and sold, the current crisis could become permanent and future generations will be hungrier – and angrier – than those of the past' (Fleshman 2008). Similar assessments of the risks to future food supplies are driving a heightened level of interest in whether the world will be able adequately to feed its population's food needs in 2050, given the impacts of global warming, combined with rising numbers of people, and a possible 'crunch' in energy supplies.[6] Most international organizations, such as the World Bank, now acknowledge that agriculture is vital for spurring overall economic growth in many poor countries. Consequently, there is renewed interest in making funding available for investment in agricultural research and development programmes.

The scale and diverse nature of climate change impacts on African food production systems imply a major set of challenges. Farmers will need to adapt by investing in alternative crops and livestock, adjusting their management regimes, storing water, and diversifying their income-generating activities, particularly from off-farm activities. Raising awareness about the possible impact of climate change, learning lessons from other areas, promoting exchange visits for farmers, and improving consultation between all levels of government and civil society will be essential. Given the high levels of uncertainty as to how overall changes will impact in particular settings, support for a bottom-up set of responses tailored to the needs and perspectives of those on the ground will be key. Working with local government, rural councils and municipal authorities will be of great importance in building an effective response that can make the most of local knowledge and priorities.

The overall impact of climate change will make certain resources, such as water, scarcer and more valuable in areas that become more arid. There will be greater competition between

Box 4.4 Building rural resilience in Burkina Faso

In the early 1980s, the central plateau of Burkina Faso was characterized by high population densities, declining cereal yields, cultivation spreading into ever more marginal land, high levels of outmigration and falling water tables. Over the last twenty years, this situation has been transformed by the widespread adoption of improved soil and water conservation activities. A range of techniques has been used: traditional planting pits (*zai*), which can rehabilitate barren land; stone lines along the contour which hold back surface run-off after rain; low permeable rock dams to help fill in gullies; and increased production and use of organic matter through establishing compost and manure pits. Today, more than 100,000 hectares of land have been treated, bringing remarkable improvements in crop yields, tree cover, rising groundwater tables, reduced outmigration and a sense of greater well-being (Reij et al. 2005).

alternative users such as pastoral herders, arable farmers, hydropower stations, irrigation systems and city dwellers. Establishing and strengthening the institutions for managing these scarce resources will be key to avoiding conflict. There is also considerable room to make better use of water for agriculture, and increase its resilience. Except for a few sites along major rivers (Nile, Niger, Zambezi), there is not much scope for further large-scale irrigation.[7] Consequently, rain-fed agriculture in Africa will remain critical for the growth of food production, with less than 5 per cent of agricultural areas under controlled irrigation at present. The most significant gains to building resilience in crop production will come from small-scale harvesting of water, particularly in rain-fed farming systems. A variety of simple systems have existed for many generations, bringing remarkable results, even in semi-arid areas, as described in Box 4.4.

Farmers have always tried to protect themselves from risk by growing a range of different crops. Those farmers facing the likelihood of increased rainfall will need to draw upon crop varieties that can withstand heavy rainfall and waterlogged soils, and invest in measures to reduce soil erosion. Research institutes around the world are tapping into the plant genetic material stored in gene banks, as well as that in wild plant species, to identify traits that can be used for adapting crops to climate change. Using traditional breeding techniques together with genetic engineering, traits such as tolerance to drought, saline soils and extreme temperatures can be incorporated into new plant varieties. For example, scientists at the International Center for Agricultural Research in the Dry Areas (ICARDA) are developing a number of wheat and barley lines able to perform well in colder winters and drier springs and summers. The task ahead is great, however. In the past few decades, the average time between scientists beginning to hunt for useful traits through to testing and having the new variety growing in farmers' fields has been forty-six years.

As always, farmers do not wait for researchers to provide the answers but continue to apply their own plant breeding knowledge in an effort to beat the risks generated by climate change. In southern Sudan, for example, women select and preserve a number of sorghum seeds from their harvests to ensure that a range of different traits are available for the next unpredictable planting season and, by doing so, are reducing risk of crop loss. More support is needed to strengthen farmer seed networks to exchange seed varieties, test out, maintain diversity and ensure local control of seed and food stocks (Rubyogo and Sperling 2009).

Genetically modified organisms (GMOs) have been seen by some as offering substantial advantages to African agriculture, in an era of climate change, with crops such as cotton, maize and soybean already developed. To date, South Africa and Burkina Faso are the only African countries to adopt commercial production of GMO crops, and there remains lively dispute over the extent to which such technologies have much to offer the smallholder sector. Those against GM technology argue that farmers need to maintain autonomy over seed supply and a diverse farming system, especially

Food

67

in an era of rising uncertainty over prices, and rainfall conditions. They also point to the risks for smallholders of depending on monopoly suppliers of seed and other agricultural inputs (Pimbert 2009; IAASTD 2009). Those in favour argue that African countries cannot afford to ignore the potential of agricultural biotechnology, but this should be seen as broader than a focus on genetic manipulation and should include a wide range of new methods for improving productivity and disease resistance in crops, livestock, fisheries and forests (Juma and Serageldin 2007; James 2004).

Forecasting weather and climate Seasonal weather forecasting can give a probability of certain weather events occurring up to three to six months in advance. It is now possible to predict with some accuracy the likelihood of events, such as drought, in parts of sub-Saharan Africa and climate variability in relation to ENSO events (Larkin and Harrison 2002). If livestock keepers know that rains will be particularly poor and pasture is likely to become scarce, they have the opportunity to sell early, before the price of livestock slumps. Equally, farmers can get guidance on the optimal time to sow and the likely demand for irrigation. Governments can prepare for adverse conditions by purchase of emergency food stocks, introducing safety nets, and distribution of inputs for the subsequent cropping season. The forecasting of longer-term climate change, although advancing rapidly, is still not sufficiently accurate, and more work is needed in translating results from macro-level climate change models into findings that can be used at smaller scales.

How does African land use affect climate change?

Globally, agriculture and land use contribute between 18 and 25 per cent of the planet's carbon emissions, much of which stems from tropical deforestation. In Africa, clearing land by 'slash and burn' of scrub and forest to make way for growing settlements, industries, agriculture and pasture, as well as deforestation for timber, is the largest source of CO_2 input to the atmosphere from the continent. Other human impacts, such as soil erosion, create sources of atmospheric dust, which influences climate variability in the region. Livestock are also significant emitters of greenhouse gases, owing to their excretion of methane. Taking the whole production chain into consideration, livestock is estimated to contribute 18 per cent of global greenhouse gas emissions.[8] Given that livestock are kept in much less intensive conditions than in Europe, China and North America, the African livestock sector is likely to have a much lower carbon footprint than industrial animal production elsewhere. Currently, the only carbon emissions from land use practices to be included in emission trading schemes concern afforestation efforts on tropical forestland. There may, however, be considerable opportunities for sequestering carbon through better land use management in the soils and vegetation found in savannah and dryland regions. Such market opportunities are discussed in the final chapter.

Conclusion

Africa hosts a very diverse set of food and farming systems, which are vulnerable in differing ways to the impacts of climate change. Overall, a high proportion of people rely on crops and livestock for a major share of their livelihoods, which means that they will be badly hit as climatic conditions worsen. Many generations of farmers have demonstrated an ability to adapt and change as the economy and environment evolve. Such adaptation has combined adoption of new crops and livestock, development of off-farm incomes, and migration to new lands. Farmers today face an uncertain future, given the scale of changes global warming is likely to bring, and the long-term neglect by governments of agricultural investment and support. Rising temperatures, shifts in rainfall, extreme events and sea level rise will all impact on productivity. Farmers will need to build more resilient systems for food, livestock and fishing, combined with better forecasting of the next season's weather and establishment of locally held food stocks. In the worst cases, people will need to move to higher-potential regions, which is of increasing difficulty given growing pressures on land.

5 | Forests

Introduction

This chapter outlines the importance of forests for incomes and produce, their role in carbon, water and biodiversity management, and how they affect and will be affected by climate change. Forests also provide a variety of intangible benefits of value to people's spiritual and recreational needs. Ownership of trees and forests raises a number of thorny issues, given the value of trees for timber and the emergence of new carbon finance under the climate change convention. Establishing and maintaining good governance of forests are vital to long-term management, and require a combination of bottom-up empowerment and top-down legal structures to frame the rights and expectations of local people and state forest agencies. For forests to play their key function in regulating global and regional climate, trees need to have a value that ensures they are 'more valuable standing than felled'.

Background

Africa hosts a rich variety of forests, from the swathes of coastal mangroves along the coastline from Angola to Senegal, and the lush rainforests of the Central African Republic and Madagascar, to the thorny savannah forests of Zambia and the majestic baobabs that populate the drylands of the Sahel. Each type of forest and woodland plays an essential role in supporting and regulating the ecosystems on which people and plants depend. Over 75 per cent of the world's usable fresh water, for example, flows through forested catchments, where it is filtered and purified. Forests provide the habitats for many thousands of plant and animal species and so help to maintain a large proportion of the world's stock of biodiversity.

Forests influence the climate through a range of physical,

chemical and biological processes that affect the atmosphere, the water cycle and global energy balance (Bonan 2008), and play two very different, but equally important, roles on the global climate stage. Their first role is that of carbon storage. Forests buffer the planet against global warming by absorbing carbon dioxide, thereby helping to stabilize the atmospheric levels of this greenhouse gas. Second, they regulate local and global weather patterns by storing and releasing moisture. Their roots bind soil and stabilize land, preventing erosion and creating natural protective barriers against the sun and storms, wind and waves, which will increase in intensity with global warming. The capacity of forests to act as an effective 'sink' for carbon will depend on how they are affected by rising temperatures and shifts in rainfall, which may lead them to die back and release large amounts of carbon dioxide into the atmosphere. Their ability to regulate local weather and water flows depends on sufficient forest cover and health being maintained.

Forests provide incomes and produce for many people, especially the poor (Capistrano 2005). They offer a reliable source of food, fuel and timber, of particular value in times of turbulent and volatile prices, enabling rural communities to provision themselves from non-market sources and thereby reduce their vulnerability. But forests are also susceptible to pressures from growing populations and commercial demands, which have resulted in the clearing of much forestland for timber, crops and infrastructure.

Africa hosts around 16 per cent of the world's forests, covering 635 million hectares (FAO 2005: 16) scattered across most of its regions except the dry Saharan belt and the desert regions of south-west Africa. The most common image of African forests is probably that of the lowland rainforests of the immense Congo basin, which stretch across central Africa and cover the Democratic Republic of Congo (DRC), parts of Gabon, Equatorial Guinea, the Central African Republic and the Republic of Congo. This is the second-largest expanse of rainforest in the world after the Amazon basin. Around 80 per cent of the species within this forest are found nowhere else in the world, highlighting the irreplaceable value of these ecosystems, in terms of biodiversity, as shown in Box 5.1. But

> ## Box 5.1 Benefits from biodiversity
>
> Cameroon's Boumba Bek National Park is a pristine rain-
> forest made up of lowland forest together with areas of
> swamp-forest and grassy savannahs that are cut through by
> swift-flowing rivers. The forest forms one of two recently
> created national parks covering an area of more than 600,000
> hectares in south-east Cameroon. The park holds rich plant
> and animal biodiversity that includes forest elephants, goril-
> las, chimpanzees, antelopes, Nile crocodiles and bongos. The
> lush vegetation provides refuge to 280 bird species, such as
> the rare Dja warbler, the Nkulengu rail and Bates's nightjar,
> while 300 species of fish, three of which are new to science,
> thrive in the park's rivers.[1]

other forest areas are also of great importance to both ecosystems
and a range of local incomes, which depend on them. The most
extensive forest lands are in the drylands of the savannah and Sahel,
which cover approximately 40 per cent of the continent.

Trees and the carbon cycle

One of the most important roles that plants and forests play
in the world's climate is in recycling carbon. Plants act as carbon
sinks by absorbing carbon dioxide (CO_2) from the atmosphere
and incorporating the carbon atoms through a process of photosynthesis into sugars and molecules that make up the plant's
woody and leaf matter, known as biomass. Plants use some of
these sugars to generate energy in a process called respiration,
which returns carbon atoms back to the atmosphere in the form
of CO_2. The remaining carbon stays locked within plants and is
released when the plant tissue breaks down.[2] This happens when
plant material is burned in forest fires and as a fuel by humans.
It also is gradually released when trees shed their leaves, or when
they die, and are attacked by microbes releasing carbon back to
the atmosphere as CO_2. The carbon stored in forest biomass, dead

wood, litter and soil together is estimated to be over 50 per cent of the global total, and more than the amount held in the form of atmospheric carbon.[3] The amount of carbon stored in forest biomass at a global level is estimated at 283 Gigatonnes (Gt). But this figure has fallen annually by 1.1 Gt, between 1990 and 2005, owing to forests being cut down.

In the absence of human activity, the carbon cycle is finely balanced, with release and absorption of carbon being more or less in equilibrium. Even though the natural system releases some twenty times more carbon into the atmosphere than human activity, this amount is usually absorbed back into tree growth within the cycle. The forest carbon cycle is far from balanced today, however, with tropical deforestation accounting for around 20 per cent of all greenhouse gas emissions associated with human activity. Different plant types store different amounts of carbon but, as a general rule of thumb, 1 cubic metre of wood stores around 0.92 tonnes of carbon.[4] In a living forest ecosystem this means that a forest in which all the trees are in a mature state can store a maximum of 350–400 tonnes of carbon per hectare (tC/ha). This old-growth state rarely occurs in real life, however, owing to natural disturbances and human intervention. Selective logging within a forest to remove the larger timber trees can reduce the carbon stock to 100–250 tC/ha, but in many cases this logging triggers a set of indirect effects that increase the carbon loss even further by, for example, opening up forests and increasing the risk of forest fires. When forests are clear-felled, the above-ground carbon stock falls almost to zero.

The rate at which a forest can absorb carbon depends on the age of the individual trees within it. A stand of relatively immature trees and vegetation acts as a carbon sink, and can accumulate carbon at a rate of 5 tC/ha/year, as the forest develops. Stands of more mature trees will absorb carbon more slowly, but even old-growth forests continue to take carbon dioxide out of the atmosphere at a significant level. This sink can be increased in size by expanding the forested area, raising the tree density and reducing levels of deforestation and degradation (Canadell and Raupach 2008).[5] Carbon flows in forestland are characterized by long periods of low

Forests

uptake, followed by short periods of rapid loss and the release of large amounts of carbon, due to harvesting and fires.

A slight increase in atmospheric CO_2 concentration has a positive effect on tree and vegetation growth up to a certain point, beyond which no further benefit is gained. It is believed that this saturation point has already been reached so that no further absorption of CO_2 by trees will be possible. There is also evidence that the role of forests as a carbon sink may reverse, as was seen in 2005, when the severe drought in the Amazon turned the forest from being a sink, able to absorb nearly two billion tonnes of CO_2, to generating more than three billion tonnes. The net impact of the drought – 5 billion extra tonnes of CO_2 in the atmosphere – exceeds the annual carbon emissions of Europe and Japan combined. As global warming increases, the balance between growth and decomposition will likely shift further, making forests less able to act as a sink in future (Global Carbon Project 2008).

The impacts of climate change on forests

Natural systems are normally resilient to a certain degree of climate variation and plant species have relied on their genetic diversity to help them evolve over many generations. Trees can adapt to long-term changes in environmental conditions by, for example, altering their pattern of growth and the timing of flowering, fruiting and germination, to fit with the new constraints. At the same time, environmental change will also alter the behaviour of other key species, such as pollinators and animals, that rely on the tree for food and shelter. But such adaptation takes time, especially in forests where the lifetime of a tree is measured in hundreds of years. A wide genetic base can give plants greater tolerance for a variety of environmental conditions. This provides the option of shifting their geographic range (Pernetta 2004), in terms of altitude or latitude, when conditions in one place no longer suit them. These adaptation processes have proved reasonably successful in the past, although fossil records show previous extinctions of plant species have occurred, primarily during periods of high climate variability (Petit et al. 2008).

The emergence of human-induced climate change, however, looks set to disturb this gradual process of adaptation. If climate change is rapid relative to the generational time of the plant, and creates conditions not previously experienced, then the change may push the species to the limits of how fast it can adapt. This will happen even more quickly if the plant species has a limited genetic range. The expectation is that the speed of global climate change over the next 100 years will put 20–30 per cent of plant and animal species at increased risk of extinction, including those within forests. These impacts will stem directly from the changes in rainfall and temperature described earlier, and from a range of other factors, such as the increased frequency and intensity of wildfires, hurricanes, insect and disease outbreaks, flooding and drought. Maintaining a broad genetic range within a given tree species, as well as a high level of biodiversity within forests as a whole, will be important factors in maintaining the resilience and productivity of forests in the face of growing pressures. Other elements in forest management to reduce vulnerability to climate change include avoiding fragmentation of forest areas, providing buffer zones, protecting mature tree stands, and establishing refuge areas (Hansen et al. 2003).

The impact of people on forests

As well as the risk to forest life posed by climate change, forests are also under attack from humans. Around four million hectares of forest are felled or burnt in Africa each year, an area equivalent to roughly twice the size of Rwanda. There are large regional differences in deforestation, with Togo having one of the highest rates, not just in Africa, but in the world, having lost 44 per cent of its forests since 1990. At a global level, average annual rates of deforestation were around 8.9 million hectares per year in the 1990s, but have slackened slightly in the last few years, with an estimated total loss of 7.3 million hectares between 2000 and 2005, largely due to substantial reforestation in parts of Europe, China and North America, which offsets losses elsewhere (FAO 2005: 16).

In Africa, as in other parts of the world, forests are cut in

Forests

favour of pasture, crops, settlements and infrastructure, and for extraction of fuel and timber, much of which is uncontrolled or under-regulated in Africa. At the global level, a rough calculation is that around 40 per cent of wood removed from forests is used as fuel, but in Africa the figure is probably double this. In Malawi, for example, charcoal use in the four largest urban areas requires the cutting and burning of an estimated 15,000 hectares of forest-land per year (Kambewa et al. 2007), from a combination of forest reserves and customary land.

The felling of tropical forests for commercial purposes is a major source of revenue for many governments and, in poorly regulated countries, for corrupt officials. In many cases, government claims ownership of forest areas, and is meant to control the issue of permits to exploit the timber. In practice, the agencies with responsibility for allocating concessions and monitoring their management are poorly staffed and have limited interest and capacity in enforcing the law. Estimates of revenue lost from illegal logging are, not unexpectedly, difficult to confirm but, in the case of Ghana, four years ago, because technically all logging was illegal, and because informal harvests paid no revenues and others failed to pay, the Ghanaian government was losing US$100 million annually. Greenpeace has estimated that non-payment of logging taxes in Gabon was worth US$12 million in 2005, while other sources estimate the proportion of timber exports of illegal origin as 50 per cent for Cameroon and 70 per cent for Gabon. Overall, the World Bank's 2004 global estimate reckons losses to be between US$5 and $15 billion (World Bank 2004). As well as the direct impacts of timber extraction in terms of loss of trees, a range of indirect impacts include the opening up of previously inaccessible territory to settlement through the construction of timber roads.

Underlying this conversion of forest land is a combination of social and economic factors, including high timber prices, popula-tion pressure and high commodity prices that make conversion profitable, with the current increase in demand for biofuel from plantations being a case in point. It is increasingly recognized that many of the drivers of deforestation are generated by consumption patterns in rich and middle-income areas, such as Europe, North America, Japan, China and India. In two of the largest deforesting countries, Brazil and Indonesia, the greater part of forest loss can be attributed to industrial agribusiness, driven by demand for palm oil, beef, soya and commercial wood products (Prince's Rainforests Project 2008). Forests in Africa are also under increasing pressure from global consumption demands, with examples of major land concessions being made for oil palm and timber felling to large agribusinesses.

The loss of forests not only represents a significant decrease in biodiversity, income and environmental services, including carbon sequestering, but it is also increasing Africa's share of CO_2 emissions. Its contribution to climate change through production of CO_2 from burning fossil fuels is very low, with sub-Saharan Africa generating less than 3 per cent of the world total. The continent does, however, make a significant contribution to the share of atmospheric CO_2 due to deforestation, forest fires and land use change (UNDP 2007/08: 313). Africa's contribution to loss of carbon from deforestation is around 25–35 per cent of the global total. As the current rate of forest replanting is only around 5 per cent of this, most of this forest area is lost for good.

The task of estimating CO_2 emissions from Africa's extensive, small-scale and mainly unregulated activities, such as wood collection and charcoal production, is fraught with difficulty, because the scale of the harvesting is not fully known and there is likely to be an underestimation of total CO_2 emission levels (Williams et al. 2007). With population expansion, industrialization and increasing land use change, Africa's CO_2 emissions are likely to grow substantially over this century. A strategy to reduce emissions will need to strike a balance between building up the carbon stock within forest systems on the one hand, and the need to cater to human and economic development on the other, which is likely to involve further loss of forest land.

Forests

Forests for livelihoods

Any change in the area of Africa's forests, or a change in the system for managing them, will have significant consequences for the millions of people who rely on them for their livelihoods. Africa's dry forests in the Sahel and savannah are inhabited by more than 230 million people (Petheram et al. 2006), many of whom are among the poorest in the world, and the importance of trees to their well-being is very great, as shown in Box 5.2. Foods collected from the forest complement the cereals that farmers grow themselves, and are an important source of vitamins and minerals, contributing to a diverse diet (ibid.). For example, in the West African savannah, many households rely on shea butter oil, which is processed from the seeds of the shea nut tree, *Butyrospermum paradoxum*, for cooking. This is the second-most important source of fat in African diets (Chege 2001), and the tree is revered locally in Benin as the 'tree of life'. The global export market for shea products is an example of a tree-based industry with a value of around US$100 million per year, with much of the collection and marketing conducted by women. There are an estimated 1,500 species of wild plants consumed in central and West Africa alone, many of which are derived from forests, representing a year-round supply of food supplements for those with access and the necessary local knowledge.

Employment and income from forests can be substantial. In the case of Uganda, for instance, it is estimated that forestry creates about 850,000 jobs, mostly in the informal sector. There are also as many as 100,000 people in full-time employment in charcoal production, plantation management, forest industries and within institutions.[6] Collection of wood for fuel, in countries such as Mozambique, provides more than 80 per cent of the country's cooking needs (Saastamoinen 2003), and supports local and international timber markets. Other income stems from the sale of forest products, such as bushmeat, firewood, medicines, thatch, fodder, medicinal plants, rattan and bamboo, craft materials and food. These products can provide vital relief at times when other sources of income, such as wage labour or farming, are hard to

Box 5.2 Trees – part of daily life in central Mali

For women in the village in Kala, central Mali, trees and the produce they supply are central to daily life, from the rope made from baobab bark, and foodstuffs based on its leaves and fruit, to the tamarind pods that add an extra sharpness to the daily porridge, and the hard *gwele* (*Prosopis*) wood whose trunk supplies the mortar for pounding millet. A woman's stool is made of *bumu*, the fast-growing *Bombax costatum*, which makes for a light, easily carved wood, and she collects a handful of *ntomono* berries (*Ziziphus mauritiana*) to chew on her way to and from the field. An infusion made from steeping a handful of leaves from the *n'galama* bush can clear a skin infection, while her hatchet cuts an armful of forage leaves from the *bala* or *Pterocarpens lucens*, as she returns home from farming.

come by. In Uganda, for example, poor households in forested areas gain up to US$75 per year from the sale of forest products.[7]

Forest products are also valuable for the national economy and have great potential for future growth. One example of this is the Tanzanian honey industry, which is supported by millions of hectares of forests and woodlands scattered throughout the country, creating an excellent habitat for bees. Production of honey and beeswax has become a small but growing source of income for rural people, with current sales of $2 million a year, and potential production value more than fifty times this.[8] The role of bees, in terms of pollinating food crops and maintaining plant biodiversity, is largely unrecognized but provides further value to the African farming sector.

The intangible benefits of forests to human spirituality, recreational needs and culture, identity and well-being are often overlooked. For indigenous people, their sense of meaning, identity and purpose in life is very closely bound up with the trees, landscape and river systems found in forest areas. In many societies, forests are thought to harbour spirits and thus require protection. The sacred groves of West Africa offer a sanctuary for many indigenous trees and bushes, which may have disappeared elsewhere, while in South Africa the National Forests Act of 1998 specifically notes the importance to its citizens of sustainable forest management for cultural, recreational and spiritual purposes.

Forest tenure

Although millions of people in sub-Saharan Africa benefit from access to forest resources, it is often these very same people who have the least say in how the forests are managed. Governments usually assert state ownership of forests, including trees in agricultural areas, on the grounds that these are assets of national importance. Thus, for example, in Guinea, Leach and Fairhead report that forestry officers continually emphasize the damage local people inflict on forests and farm trees, yet are blind to the increase in forest cover that farmers have brought about over recent decades. The narrative of environmental degradation espoused by forestry staff then justifies their role in taking control of the management of natural resources, and 'deeming villagers to be incapable and destructive resource custodians' (Leach and Fairhead 1997).

This assertion of state-held rights runs into several practical difficulties, however, owing to the inability of forest agencies to manage forests effectively, the risks of corruption associated with the issue of timber permits, and the lack of incentive for local people to protect local forest resources. Finding ways to strengthen local rights to govern forests is key to creating the right incentives for their long-term management and to strengthen their role in mitigating global warming. Limited progress is being made in this direction, and mainly outside dense tropical forest. For example, joint forest management systems have developed in southern Africa, bringing together community and government interests to look after woodlands and wildlife, with a share of revenue kept by village committees. In Ethiopia, the government has started to recognize the role that local groups can play in reforesting degraded land, if they have long-term-use rights. And in West Africa, a growing number of local 'conventions' have been agreed between people and government to transfer rights and responsibilities for woodlands and fisheries to local management groups. Nevertheless, governments have retained powers over high-value tropical forestland, because of the considerable revenues generated by the sale of timber permits.

Forests and carbon management

As discussed earlier, deforestation represents a significant source of atmospheric carbon. Yet emissions from tropical deforestation were barely included in the Kyoto protocol, agreed in 1997. The decision to exclude forest-sector emissions was based on the premise that the uncertainties associated with quantifying GHG emissions within this sector would weaken the overall strength of the climate change treaty. Developing countries, many of which benefit economically from their forest resources, were also worried that a plan to reduce deforestation would threaten their right to exploit their forests. The one exception to this, so far, is the Clean Development Mechanism (CDM), whereby industrialized countries are able to earn carbon credits from paying for reforestation and afforestation projects in the developing world (Santilli et al. 2005). The actual take-up of projects has, however, been negligible to date. Given that deforestation accounts for up to 20 per cent of carbon emissions worldwide, and with a great proportion of this taking place in developing countries, the need for a financial mechanism to reduce deforestation is gaining recognition. With negotiations in process for a post-Kyoto agreement to start after 2012, there is rapidly growing interest in setting up a scheme to compensate countries for avoided deforestation. This scheme is aimed at Reduced Emissions from Deforestation and Degradation (REDD) and oriented towards developing countries.[9]

Proposals for a REDD scheme essentially offer a payment for provision of a global environmental service, which takes the form of the sequestering of carbon by forest trees, thereby reducing the amount of carbon in the atmosphere. This can be achieved in several ways – by maintaining the existing forest area, stopping

81

deforestation, and planting to increase the density of trees, in order to boost the carbon storage capacity per hectare. It can also be done by keeping trees that already exist alive for longer through, for instance, allowing more time before harvesting, as well as employing better fire management and pest control measures (Nabuurs et al. 2007). As well as the carbon storage benefits, avoided deforestation also generates a range of additional services, including conservation of biodiversity, soil stabilization and water filtration, which in turn reduce vulnerability to climate change.

The potential for REDD schemes to contribute substantially to addressing climate change depends, however, on whether the forest carbon protected from deforestation will persist over the coming decades in the face of changes in temperature and rainfall, as well as continuing pressures to exploit the timber resource. It is also possible that successful actions in one country will displace the pressure to harvest trees elsewhere, so that there is no net global benefit. Numerous initiatives are now under way to launch REDD schemes, through bodies such as the World Bank, with its Forest Carbon Partnership Facility, the Prince of Wales's Rainforests Project, and the Norwegian government's Forest Fund. At the climate change conference in Poznan in December 2008, more than nine hundred people took part in debates about forest management and its potential for addressing climate change, demonstrating the high level of interest now associated with REDD. It is likely that some form of avoided deforestation payment mechanism will be an integral part of the post-Kyoto climate agreement due to be finalized in Copenhagen, although the practical details of how it would work in-country will need subsequent elaboration.

How might a payments mechanism work?

Under a REDD scheme, payment is based on the value of the carbon in existing trees. It is estimated that cutting global deforestation by half could cost between $17 and $33 billion per year, which compares favourably with more expensive ways to cut greenhouse gas emissions (Eliasch Review 2008). This value is based on a set of assumptions about carbon prices, and the opportunity cost forgone from avoided deforestation, such as the loss of potential revenue from growing oil palm for biofuel (Kanninen et al. 2007). This sum is equivalent to around 15 per cent of the official development assistance flows currently received by developing countries in 2005 (EarthTrends 2008). The question is whether this amount is sufficient to compensate for the loss of income that these countries would otherwise have gained from granting concessions, timber sales and converting forests to other uses, such as farming. The basic assumption driving a REDD scheme is that forests need to be more valuable standing than felled. But it needs to be asked – 'more valuable to whom?' Standing forest may well be more valuable to forest dwellers than seeing their land cleared, but they are rarely in a position to decide. Conversely, standing forest may be worth much less to a forestry official than when it is felled, since he can gain from the issue of timber permits.

There are, therefore, many challenges to building a strong and equitable market-based REDD policy (Saunders 2007), given the weak institutions responsible for managing forests and associated systems of governance. Serious concerns have been raised about the distribution of funding from such a scheme, and the share to be gained by national and local government coffers, as opposed to local people. Equally, there are risks that forest land will become more valuable as a result of the REDD scheme, and more powerful groups will seek to displace forest dwellers in order to reap the REDD rewards. In a global context where commodity prices are highly volatile, it is unclear at what level the REDD payment should be pitched. If it is too low, relative to the gains to be made from soya bean and oil palm, then it will not act as an incentive to stop further forest clearance.

The functioning of any REDD scheme requires more work to address some of the practical difficulties. The carbon stock in a given forest system needs to be estimated, but accurately assessing forest biomass is not easy. The rate of biomass production and therefore carbon sequestration are related to the speed of tree growth and density of trees, and these in turn are dependent on factors such as the tree species, local climatic conditions and

83

how the trees are managed. There will be uneven benefits from REDD schemes across Africa, because tree growth, and therefore biomass production, in relatively humid areas is much greater than in more arid areas. Recent work in the Sahel shows that even these drylands can act as significant carbon sinks, because of the very extensive areas involved. A conservative estimate for carbon sequestration in the woodlands of the Sahel gives a figure of 20 tonnes of carbon per hectare, based on the tree mass. Including the below-ground carbon and grassland elements would increase the volume associated with the restoration of woodlands in the Sahel. If carbon is priced at $10 per tonne, this would generate the equivalent of $200 per hectare. Reij reckons an area of 5 million hectares in Niger has already undergone this improvement, equal to $1 billion worth of carbon (Reij 2008).

There is also the risk that carbon markets will encourage the choice of fast-growing tree monocultures in place of a more diverse range of forest species, if they conserve more carbon per area. But this would reduce the important biodiversity benefits, which are not given a price by REDD schemes.

'Leakage' of carbon is also a risk, as when deforestation is re-duced in one region or country, but this merely displaces demand to another region. Equally, those seeking farmland may move from a well-protected area to somewhere with fewer restrictions. The scheme also requires that there is a workable definition of a 'forest'. Although this may initially seem an easy task, an inappropriate label has great significance as it determines which forests can be included in or excluded from the scheme that pays for avoided deforestation. Any programmes involving avoided deforestation and reforestation rely on knowing the area of forest and estima-ting the value of the carbon stock present within the forest being defined.

The power of forests to sequester carbon is one important eco-system attribute. But there are also many other functions provided by forests, such as their harbouring of biodiversity, protection of watersheds and provision of moisture to local weather systems. Recent research suggests that the carbon sequestration element

accounts for less than 30 per cent of the total environ[...]
associated with reduced deforestation. Hence, if the p[...]
other environmental services were to be factored into [...]
mechanism, the value of standing forests would be c[...]
greater.

Conclusion

This chapter has argued that controlling deforestation is a key element in addressing global climate change. Yet the countries with the highest REDD potential in Africa score very poorly on governance measures, which is why they are currently failing to control deforestation. The availability of carbon finance will do little to generate more sustainable management of forested land unless the fundamental problems inherent in rights and enforcement are addressed. As Oksanen notes, 'How can a country that does not control forest crime (illegal logging, arson, illegal conversion) enter into a credible contract ...' (2007). This will require revision of laws and regulations, institutional reforms, forest information and transparency, and national plans to combat illegal logging and other forest crime.

Forests are vital for many people's livelihoods, yet local people rarely have rights recognized by law to manage and control these resources. A clearer framework of incentives is needed for long-term management of forest areas, a strengthening of buffer zones around forests, systems to minimize fragmentation of existing forests, and improved monitoring for pests and fires. People in government and civil society working on climate change need to communicate and collaborate with those involved in the forestry, biodiversity and environmental sectors (Vermeulen 2006; Macqueen and Vermeulen 2006). National platforms, such as the Forest Governance Learning Groups, offer one means to help make this collaboration effective.

Forests in Africa are becoming an increasingly global commodity, whether as providers of carbon services for addressing climate change, or as raw materials for timber, fuel or pulp. Rich consumers have the power to help shift forest management along

.e sustainable paths by seeking products that are clearly labelled as stemming from a sustainably managed forest. Equally, a REDD payments mechanism has the potential to secure the future for large areas of standing trees and the forest dwellers dependent on them. But these gains will come about only if time and effort are invested in clarifying and enforcing rights of access and use, and finding the best means to distribute the proceeds from REDD among local people, local government and national authorities. Neither an exclusively top-down nor a bottom-up approach is likely to work; rather a combination will be needed of local empowerment and national support (Prince's Rainforests Project 2008). Tackling some of the powerful forces behind deforestation, such as logging companies, pressures for infrastructural development and conversion of forests to agribusiness, will require concerted action on an unprecedented scale in many countries (Cotula and Mayers 2009).

6 | Cities[1]

Introduction

This chapter describes how human settlements are changing and developing in many parts of Africa, and the widespread prevalence of urban poverty, such that often more than two-thirds of the urban population live in informal squatter settlements. Vulnerable to multiple risks, such as from demolition and extortionate rents, they are also sited in areas most at risk from floods, poor water supply and pollution. Cities are particularly at risk from climate change because many city governments lack the information and resources to cope. A more proactive approach is needed, which builds resilience into city plans rather than reacting to disasters once they have happened. Investments need to be made in all-weather roads, better water, sanitation and drainage systems, low-cost housing in safe sites, and good provision for healthcare and emergency response. Global warming will generate a range of problems, including heatwaves, flooding, pollution and sea level rise. Municipal governments have much to learn from each other, as each prepares its own plan for adaptation. Successful, well-governed cities greatly reduce climate-related risks for low-income populations; unsuccessful, badly governed cities will greatly increase such risks. Thus, questions of responsive and representative city government are key to ensuring a response to climate change hazards which work for the majority.

Growing cities

Urbanization is proceeding apace in most middle- and low-income countries around the world. The year 2008 marked the tipping point in human history at which more than half of the world's population live in urban areas. And it is reckoned that over the next thirty years, more than 90 per cent of global population

TABLE 6.1 Level of urbanization for different regions, 1950–2010 (percentage of total population)

Africa and its regions	1950	1970	1990	2010
Sub-Saharan Africa	11.1	19.5	28.2	37.3
Eastern Africa	5.3	10.4	17.9	23.7
Middle Africa	14.0	24.9	32.5	42.9
Northern Africa	24.8	36.3	44.7	52.0
Southern Africa	37.6	43.7	48.8	58.8
Western Africa	9.9	21.4	33.2	44.6

Source: UN (2008); note that figures for 2010 are projections

growth will be in the small and large cities of the developing world. The African continent is no stranger to these trends, although to date most countries do not yet have half their peoples living in urban areas. Table 6.1 shows changes in the levels of urbanization in different regions of Africa over recent decades.

In 1950, there were only two cities in Africa with more than one million inhabitants; by the year 2000 this had increased to thirty-seven (Satterthwaite et al. 2007), and by 2010 is likely to reach fifty-two. Urban growth in Africa is not just a story of large cities getting ever more enormous, however. There are many small and medium-sized towns that attract permanent and temporary residents, and which play a vital role as catalysts for economic growth in their particular district. Many of these towns are of long standing, having grown up in the pre-colonial period as major centres of trade and government, such as Kano in northern Nigeria, Kumasi in Ghana and Timbuktu in Mali. Others were established as administrative centres for the colonial authorities, such as Harare in Zimbabwe, Nairobi in Kenya and Entebbe in Uganda. And since the 1950s, a new set of urban areas has developed around major ports, such as Tema in Ghana, and new capitals such as Abuja, Nigeria, and Dodoma, Tanzania.

Urban migration and the growth of cities have often been seen as a problem that needs to be controlled. But cities are central to successful economies, which are heavily dependent on having well-functioning urban centres. At their best, urban centres provide a vital point of integration into the world economy, with investment and economic activity creating multiple jobs and opportunities. The outcome of growing cities depends very much on how the process is managed, however – it can bring either great benefit or extreme hardship for those who are drawn to them. With good management and planning, cities offer the benefits of economies of scale and proximity and can provide their concentrated population with safe access to water and sanitation services, a supply of power, access to healthcare, education and markets. Well-designed cities rely on planning, with building codes to ensure housing is constructed on sound foundations and with access to public transport. But in many cities, millions of people are confined to dense and dangerous shanty towns, where they live in unplanned, often home-made housing that is precariously situated, with little or no access to basic amenities, such as water and sanitation. They lack the political representation they need to demand change and are desperately poor.

Over half of the urban population of Angola, Chad, Madagascar, Malawi, Mozambique, Niger and Sierra Leone live below the poverty line, and urban populations in Zambia, Burundi, the Gambia, Kenya and Zimbabwe are not far behind. Rural poverty is one of the reasons people seek out an alternative, and hopefully better, life in the cities, but in many instances the scale of this urban migration is greater than the ability of the city authorities to provide amenities and opportunities. This means that the expanding cities of the future, such as Gaborone, described in Box 6.1, are likely to be composed mainly of poor people, and the current impoverishment of urban life has become a huge challenge to development in Africa (UNFPA 2007).

For the majority of city dwellers, who live in squatter settlements, the situation is harsh. They lack formal tenure rights and are very vulnerable to having their shacks demolished by the municipal authorities to make way for new infrastructure, commercial development or in response to pressure from the middle classes. Many

Box 6.1 Gaborone, the growing capital of Botswana

Gaborone illustrates many of the challenges faced by rapidly growing towns. Since 1971, the city's population has jumped from 17,700 to more than 186,000 people in 2007, and is expected to reach 500,000 by the year 2020. The city now exhibits a low-density sprawl, high unemployment rates, a 47 per cent poverty rate and a large informal sector. The high HIV/AIDS prevalence rates combine with poor water supply and sanitation to render the majority increasingly vulnerable to premature death (UNPFA 2007).

squatters find themselves at the mercy of landlords who demand exorbitant rents. Water supplies are hopelessly inadequate, so they must purchase water from sellers, at prices per litre far greater than that paid by richer neighbours, who gain access to water through the public piped supply system. They also use polluted water for many domestic tasks because water from vendors or kiosks is too expensive for this. With very limited investment in sanitation, conditions are dirty and dangerous to health. Many urban households have to share toilets that are of poor quality; it is common for plastic bags to become a substitute for public toilets; as they are thrown away, these are known as 'flying' toilets. Haphazard building on slopes and in gulleys has disrupted the pattern of water flow, so that storms bring floods to many urban areas, causing great damage as well as added risks from waterborne diseases.

While few detailed assessments have been made of climate change impacts on urban areas in Africa, it is likely, given the existing gulf between infrastructural provision and current need, that those people most vulnerable today will find themselves at even greater risk in future (IPCC 2007: ch. 9). The biggest threats from climate variability and change stem from shifts in temperature, rainfall patterns, sea level rise, and an increase in extreme weather events (ibid.). There are, however, more subtle ways in which cities and their populations will be affected by climate, and in turn have an influence on the climate, as described below. In addition, urban areas will be affected by the many other global trends and changes under way, such as those relating to the cost of fuel and basic foodstuffs.

The impact of cities on the environment

Urban centres have multiple interactions with the wider environment in which they are situated. Worldwide, urban centres occupy just 2 per cent of the total land surface of the earth, yet their populations and enterprises consume 75 per cent of the planet's natural resources. Consequently, their influence on the global ecosystem is very significant, for good or ill. Cities are reckoned to generate around 40 per cent of global greenhouse gases, although accounting for around 70 per cent of all CO_2 emissions from fossil fuel use. Middle- and high-income urban dwellers have very different consumption patterns to poor people in cities, and they also consume more energy for electricity, cooking and heating than rural populations. Cities in Africa have higher greenhouse gas emissions per person than rural areas, although their per capita figures are far below those in Europe and North America.

Urban centres also have multiple interactions with their surroundings, for instance as they expand over agricultural land and as city wastes pollute water bodies. Poorly managed and degraded urban transport and energy systems have a range of adverse impacts, from health problems to deterring new investment. Many of the effects of urban areas on the environment are not necessarily linear; larger cities do not always lead to larger environmental problems, while small urban areas may generate substantial damage. But the economic power of urban dwellers also provides many benefits, such as a market for goods and services provided from the neighbouring and more distant rural hinterland, generating positive feedbacks to food producers, craft-makers and migrant labourers.

The health of urban populations in Africa depends on achieving a better balance between the urban area and its broader hinterland. Expanding cities can create a host of potential negative impacts. The use of land and water by urban centres changes the environment around them (McGranahan et al. 2007). They encroach into valuable ecosystems through housing developments, over-exploitation of natural resources and erosion of ecosystem services. The demarcation of administrative boundaries also makes it difficult for the broader ecosystem to be managed most effectively. Weak communication between government officials and surrounding urban areas can exacerbate problems. Watershed management, for example, is normally outside a city planner's jurisdiction, but the urban areas will be affected by decisions on water allocation or flood control measures that are made upstream. So, communication between these local authorities and an understanding of ecosystem flows are imperative. Most of these environmental problems stem from limitations in city staffing, resources and governance. Better-governed cities can be far healthier for their populations and also reduce the environmental costs they generate in their hinterlands and beyond.

In most African urban centres, 40–60 per cent of inhabitants live below the poverty line,[2] and as many of these poor people cannot afford to buy their basic needs in markets, they turn to resources from the environment. For instance, urban agriculture (including livestock) is an important source of food and income for many African urban households. For the poorer inhabitants of Ghana's capital Accra, the biodiversity of the adjacent rural areas, and in particular the large Sakumo wetlands, provides many resources that are vital to their livelihoods and well-being. The wetlands provide fishing and materials, such as raffia for cottage industries and income generation, herbs for traditional medicine, and dry-season vegetable gardens.[3] Accra's residents also rely on forests and rivers for fuels, such as charcoal, and for hydropower. The natural environment supplies services such as flood control, clean water and a green belt of woodland to regulate the micro-climate in the city. These 'free' services are vital to the health and safety of the city but are often overlooked by urban dwellers and city planners.

The boundary between urban and rural areas, and between urban and rural dwellers, is often blurred in practice. People combine an urban life with continued reliance on land and livestock held in rural areas. In the case of Gaborone, Botswana, as in many other African cities, many of the urban poor rely on cattle and cropland in their home areas for some of their food and income, especially when urban life gets tough (Tacoli 2007). Equally, the flux of migration shifts over time as circumstances change. In Côte d'Ivoire, the economic downturn in the mid-1990s led many young men to return to their family land to re-establish a farming existence. On their return home, many found that their elders had sold their land to incomers from the north, and from neighbouring Burkina Faso and Mali, leaving them with much-reduced prospects for establishing their own farm. The scale of this 'de-urbanization' for particular regions during economic downturns is certainly underestimated (Potts 2009).

Cities at risk

By their very nature, cities concentrate people and their homes, roads and motor vehicle traffic, industrial activity, trade and wastes. If well managed, they present thriving, dynamic yet sustainable places for people to live and work. If poorly planned and managed, cities can be dangerous places, their populations made vulnerable to extreme weather events that have the potential for disaster. Infrastructure is at risk from climate change in different ways and to different degrees, depending on its state of development, resilience and adaptability. In general, floods and storms bring about more physical damage, while drought and heatwaves have a more indirect impact on infrastructure systems (IPCC 2007: ch. 7). But populations are even more vulnerable if there is no infrastructure. A very large proportion of Africa's urban population lives in informal or illegal settlements lacking storm and surface drains, all-weather roads, piped water and provision for sanitation.

Most city and municipal governments face a grave handicap in that their responsibilities far outweigh their resources. They lack the information needed to address climate-related risks, such as maps and household data about current populations, as well as data on possible future scenarios. This lack of forward planning

Cities

93

makes large sections of the urban population more exposed to a range of hazards linked to climate change, which will increase the frequency and intensity of storms, floods and heatwaves, and the risk of disease, constraints on water supplies and a rise in food prices (Satterthwaite et al. 2007). The key to planning in relation to climate change is to understand how urban development exacerbates risk, and to take action to build greater resilience and adaptation into city-wide and local community plans (ibid.).

Cities concentrate people and markets, and generate much higher land prices than rural areas. As a result, low-income groups are usually forced to seek housing alternatives outside the control of official land and building regulators. This also means that they will be excluded from the regulatory framework designed to protect tenants' rights, creating a situation that allows abuse by landlords. The combination of illegal settlements and lack of rights for inhabitants results in people living in overcrowded and badly designed settlements in high-risk areas that block natural drainage channels and sit precariously on steep hillsides and flood plains, making them prone to floods, landslides, fires and storms (ibid.). The scale of urban expansion and unregulated development taking place in Nigeria's capital, Lagos, described in Box 6.2, is a case in point. Most of the risk to poor urban dwellers is associated with the incapacity of local governments to ensure provision for infrastructure and disaster risk reduction. Local government also renders squatter citizens more vulnerable because of their refusal to work with the inhabitants of 'illegal settlements', even when a third or more of the population live there.

The concentration of people, finance and enterprise in cities should bring greater economies of scale and proximity, and hence lower per capita costs for service provision, and measures to reduce risk, such as better drainage, or setting up an early warning system. The costs of supporting disaster response are also proportionally lower per head of population, compared to less densely settled areas (Satterthwaite et al. 2007).

A number of new initiatives have been set up to provide support to the urban poor. In many African nations, there are federations

Box 6.2 Lagos – urban growth and vulnerability

Lagos is one of Africa's largest cities and has also been one of the world's fastest-growing cities over the last few decades. The most recent UN estimates suggest it will have 12.4 million inhabitants by 2015. Official neglect and corruption, poor governance, extreme poverty and rapid population growth, combined with the geographic disadvantage of being less than two metres above sea level, make the population of Lagos extremely vulnerable to the negative effects of climate change.

The impact of sea level rise will be felt most strongly by the poorest, who live in sprawling settlements of shacks built on stilts above the water, in areas at highest risk of flooding. Badly designed roads lack gutters for drainage, and poor planning means that buildings have been constructed across waterways, and now block storm-water run-off. The lack of municipal waste collection means rubbish stagnates and blocks drainage channels; inadequate sewer coverage (much of Lagos lacks sewers) and water treatment infrastructure compounds the risk of pollution spreading during floods and slows recovery. Any increase in the intensity of storms and storm surges will multiply the extreme difficulties that Lagos currently experiences. Increasing temperatures will aggravate the problems associated with local air pollution from traffic congestion and industry, and increase the risk of heat-stress-related deaths.

Beginning to tackle climate change is a mammoth task for a city such as Lagos. It needs to begin with financial and technical assistance and be carried out in tandem with reducing existing poverty levels, planning for future risks and implementing environmental protection measures (British Council 2004; Satterthwaite et al. 2007; Aina 1995; Aina and Andoh 2003; Adeyinka Sunday and Taiwo Olalekan 2006; Nwafor 1986).

formed by the urban poor or homeless that are now working with local NGOs and local governments in slum and squatter upgrading, in new residential developments and in providing or improving infrastructure – for instance, in South Africa, Namibia, Malawi, Zimbabwe, Tanzania and Ghana. The right to land tenure is important for security and necessary for building a resilient community.[4]

Air pollution

Even under current climate conditions, air pollution is emerging as a key health threat to urban Africans, but this is mostly from indoor air pollution with effects being felt disproportionately by the poor, the elderly and children.[5] The burning of fuel wood and charcoal is usually very inefficient, and pollution from indoor smoke is reckoned to cause 1.5 million deaths per year. Outside the home, fumes from motor vehicles, traffic jams and poorly tuned engines combine with emissions generated by a range of industrial concerns to create a smog of different chemicals.[6] Levels of many pollutants, such as ozone, are affected by atmospheric conditions and tend to be higher on warmer days and, although evidence from developing-country cities is weak, research elsewhere suggests that there are significant air pollution risks associated with rising temperatures. Urban air pollution also has an impact beyond city boundaries as pollution is found on crops far away from the city.

Heat island effect

City environments can create a phenomenon known as the 'heat island' effect whereby, within particular parts of the city, the temperature remains higher than in the surroundings. For cities that already experience temperatures that are sufficiently high to create heat stress, those who live in these 'heat islands' face more serious problems. Heat islands also trap atmospheric pollutants, with associated health implications for urban populations. The predicted increase in global temperatures due to climate change provides added cause for concern by intensifying temperatures within cities even further, unless measures are taken to mitigate the effects. Appropriate building design, provision for public space and greening of cities with vegetation can lower local temperatures, as well as providing shade.

The warmer environment created by cities can mean that cloudiness and fog occur more often; rainfall can be 5–10 per cent higher in cities, and there are more frequent thunderstorms and hailstorms. Studies for the city of Ouagadougou in Burkina Faso point to the beneficial effect of the green belt of trees in the heart of the city, which helps offset the rise in temperature associated with increased urbanization (Offerle et al. 2005). The impact of greater levels of urbanization combined with climate change is expected to raise urban temperatures even further and will exacerbate existing heat island effects.

Heatwaves

Although heatwaves are not specifically urban events, their impact is made considerably worse owing to the urban heat island effect. Heatwaves have been associated with a rise in mortality, an increased strain on infrastructure, such as energy, water and transport, and a rise in social disturbance. Some impacts are indirect, affecting revenue from tourism, the retail sectors and ecosystem services. Not everyone is so vulnerable to heat stress, and those most affected are the very young, the elderly, those with pre-existing ailments, the immobile and the economically disadvantaged (McGregor et al. 2007).

Heatwaves are largely ignored as a natural hazard and their health, economic and social impacts on society are poorly researched at present (ibid.). The most recent heatwave to hit Europe in 2003, causing 35,000 deaths over a two-week period, highlighted the need for society to prepare itself for and cope more effectively with heatwaves. This is even more important in the context of a warming climate and increasingly variable temperatures, which are expected to bring more frequent heatwaves. In Europe, milder winter temperatures will compensate for mortality caused by hotter summers, but poor populations in African cities gain no such compensation (Campbell-Lendrum and Corvalán 2007).

One means of coping with heatwaves is obviously to rely more on

97

air conditioning, but this has the downside of contributing further emissions (unless drawing electricity from renewable sources). More sustainable options include changing the design of urban architecture and planning, in ways that encourage building in cooler, shady and more breezy spaces. An early warning system for weather and seasonal climate forecasting needs to be established and tied in with strategies to reduce the impact of heatwaves on the most vulnerable.

Rainfall and run-off

Floods have long caused serious disasters for many African cities, but flooding is becoming increasingly serious and common, with larger impacts, as can be seen in Box 6.3. Urbanization almost always means a large increase in the proportion of the land that is impermeable. The compaction of soil and the hard surface of roads and buildings prevent the infiltration of rainwater into the ground. Run-off therefore occurs more rapidly, and the channelling of surface water into drains within cities creates more intense and rapid peak flows. During heavy rainfall this increases the risk of flooding, which can cause damage to city infrastructure (British Council 2004). Floods are also responsible for spreading pollutants and debris within the affected urban area as well as farther afield, creating health and environmental problems.

Water supplies

A high proportion of the urban population in sub-Saharan Africa lack water piped to their home, nor do they have provision for the removal of waste water. Many have to rely on public standpipes with intermittent supplies, poor-quality water and long queues. Or they have to purchase water from kiosks or vendors – but such water is too expensive to meet all their needs, so they draw on polluted water from rivers or shallow wells.

In general, as cities get larger, they increasingly draw on water sources from outside their confines. In some cases, water is brought a great distance, as in the case of Johannesburg, South Africa, which relies on reservoirs established in Lesotho, some 114 kilometres

Box 6.3 Flooding in African cities

Flooding is becoming an increasingly severe and more frequent problem in cities in Africa, with the impacts particularly felt by the urban poor. Climate change is aggravating flooding problems by altering rainfall patterns, tending to increase storm frequency and intensity. But, in most cities, local changes are greatly increasing flood risk by restricting where floodwaters can go, as large parts of the ground are covered with settlements, roads and pavements, and natural channels are obstructed. These mean increased local run-off and higher flood frequency, magnitude and duration. Flooding is aggravated by the occupation of flood plains, usually by informal settlements, and the lack of attention to household waste collection, and to the construction and maintenance of drainage channels. Now, even quite modest storms produce high flows in rivers or drains, and floods.

Four different types of flooding are evident: localized flooding due to inadequate drainage; flooding from small streams whose catchment areas lie almost entirely within the built-up area; flooding from major rivers on whose banks urban areas are built; and coastal flooding from the sea or through a combination of high tides and high river flows from inland watersheds. Localized flooding occurs many times a year in many informal settlements, because there are few drains (or those that exist are blocked), most of the ground is highly compacted and pathways between dwellings become streams after heavy rain (Douglas et al. 2008).

distant, or the reliance of Dakar on the Lac de Guiers in Senegal. Most cities in Africa rely on a combination of rivers, wells tapping into groundwater and water brought from dams upstream.

Climate change will affect the availability of water from all these sources, in a number of ways. Municipal water storage systems are usually planned according to anticipated need based on population

Cities

and average rainfall forecasts, and have built in extra capacity to cope with slight variations in these factors. The water supply can become stretched when rainfall is exceptionally low, which reduces stored water, and can also have environmental implications, such as allowing saltwater intrusion into the lower reaches of a river or into aquifers. This risk is particularly high for coastal cities, as can be seen in the case of Beira in Mozambique, which must now extend its 50-kilometre pumping system a further 5 kilometres inland to locate fresh water (Wilbanks and Romero Lankao 2007).

Water stress during times of drought can also be created by in-equalities in the distribution system. As well as servicing domestic water requirements, rivers also supply water for agriculture and industry and, during times of water scarcity, allocation decisions will favour one sector over another. For example, local farmers must compete with Dakar's inhabitants for water from the Lac de Guiers in Senegal. There is also the factor of distance from source to be considered. Water supply systems, such as those for large coastal cities, are often downstream of other major users and so are the first to suffer when rivers dry up (ibid.). A reduction in average stream flow also results in an increase in the unit cost of water, and treatment of waste water. Low availability of water for drinking and sanitary purposes can trigger outbreaks of diarrhoea and, in extreme cases, cholera. Water shortages also affect the generation of hydroelectric power (Muller 2007).

Increased temperatures and changes in rainfall will increase the demand for water for drinking, for cooling systems and for the urban environment, including parks, playgrounds, trees and gardens (Wilbanks and Romero Lankao 2007). If climate change causes the failure of small local water sources, such as hand-dug wells, and triggers urban migration, then regional water supplies will need to expand to cope with population growth. At the other extreme, flooding in urban areas can create further problems by damaging treatment works and municipal infrastructure (British Council 2004).

It has been estimated that the costs of adapting existing urban water infrastructure to climate change in Africa are US\$1.05–2.65

billion annually. This includes water storage, waste-water treatment and electricity generation (Muller 2007). These figures, however, do not take account of the fact that a high proportion of the urban population currently has no access to water and sanitation systems. For them, there is no infrastructure to be adapted. Hence, the true cost of adaptation should include the costs of building adequate water and drainage systems to cope with current and future urban needs (ibid.).

Coastal cities

Humans have a long history of settling on coastlines, and ports such as Mombasa on Kenya's coast and Alexandria in Egypt have been centres of trade for many centuries, generating economic wealth and opportunities (McGranahan et al. 2007). Compared to other regions of the world, only 1 per cent of Africa's coastal land is less than ten metres above sea level, and only 12 per cent of its urban population resides in this zone (ibid.).

This figure varies between regions, however, depending on the population and geography. In West Africa, the situation is more extreme, with 40 per cent of the population living in coastal cities. For some countries, such as Senegal, almost two-thirds of the population live in the Dakar coastal area and about 90 per cent of industry is also located in this zone, which lies less than 10 metres above sea level. Much of Saint Louis, Senegal's second-largest city, is less than a metre above mean sea level. Heading east along the coast, it is expected that by 2020 the coastline from Accra in Ghana to the Niger delta will be one 500-kilometre-long continuous urban settlement of 50 million people. In Benin, as in most other coastal nations, a high proportion of the population and the largest city are on the coast. In Benin's case, half the nation's population (over three million inhabitants) lives on the coast, in the capital Cotonou and surrounding areas. The coastal location is vital to Cotonou's economy, which is heavily reliant on its import-export trade. But this coastal region is vulnerable to sea level rise, with potentially catastrophic impacts on the economy, the population and natural systems (Dossou and Gléhouenou-Dossou 2007). The situation is much the same in other regions of Africa where strategic coastal settlements and ports are at risk. For Eritrea, a 1-metre rise in sea level would likely cause damage of over US$250 million as a result of the submergence of infrastructure and other economic installations in Massawa, one of the country's two port cities (IPCC 2007: ch. 9).

The range of impacts on coastal cities is great and includes: sea level rise, flood risk due to the flow of floodwater or rainwater run-off, changes in the water table, decreased quality or quantity of groundwater due to saltwater intrusion, and erosion of beaches and protective barriers due to an increase in storm intensity and larger waves (British Council 2004). Many coasts are already experiencing erosion and ecosystem losses, but few studies have unambiguously quantified the relationships between observed coastal land loss and sea level rise (IPCC 2007: ch. 6).

Many of Africa's largest cities are on the coast, and will face serious problems with sea level rise and storm surges. Alexandria is particularly at risk; a 0.5-metre rise would directly affect more than two million people in the city, with $35 billion losses to land, property and infrastructure, as well as incalculable losses of historic and cultural assets.[7]

The population exposed to flooding by storm surges will increase over the twenty-first century. The concentration of populations and economic activities in low-lying coastal areas means that a high number of people will be exposed (McGranahan et al. 2007). The East African region, and in particular countries such as Mozambique, are likely to suffer from a combination of tropical-storm landfalls and large projected population growth, in addition to sea level rise (IPCC 2007: ch. 6).

Combining this vulnerability with high levels of urban poverty and insufficient urban planning means that a large number of people risk losing their homes and livelihoods. Sea level rise and storm surges can also cause damage to settlements well above the high-water level, and the social and economic impacts of damage to the coast will be felt far inland, as climate change impacts spread from directly impacted areas and sectors to other areas and sectors through extensive and complex linkages (Satterthwaite et al. 2007). Rising sea levels may make the infrastructure of water treatment plants and power stations obsolete and, rather than altering the infrastructure, cities at high risk may need to relocate to upland areas, though this would cost billions of dollars (British Council 2004).

Fires

Aside from the direct impact of climate change in terms of increase in heat stress and erratic water availability, other effects on urban areas are more indirect. With low rainfall, lower relative humidity and higher wind speeds come the likelihood of an increase in the frequency and intensity of wildfires. When this is combined with rapid urban growth, especially in informal settlements, the exposure of poor families to personal and infrastructure loss due to fires increases. In the city of Cape Town more than 41,000 informal homes were damaged or destroyed in fires between 1990 and 2004. Increased firefighting capacity and better urban design are needed, such as construction of firebreaks between residential areas and vegetation.

Cities

Balancing adaptation and mitigation

Successful, well-governed cities greatly reduce climate-related risks for low-income populations; unsuccessful, badly governed cities do not and may greatly increase such risks. Land-use planning and regulations influence the supply of land for housing and its price, and hence the ability of poorer urban households to buy, build or rent good-quality, legal accommodation in areas that are not at risk from floods or landslides. Advanced planning to adapt to climate change relies on governments having the capacity to implement and police regulations that support land-for-housing development, improve housing conditions and widen the housing available for low-income households. Improved housing and infrastructure for low-income populations also need flexibility in government practices as in, for instance, Windhoek, where the city authorities worked with the Namibian Homeless People's Federation to amend land-use and infrastructure standards so homes could be afforded by low-income groups (Muller and Mitlin 2007). But these are the exceptions, as are the political conditions that produced them (Satterthwaite et al. 2007).

Cities will have an important role in slowing and eventually stopping global warming. As most greenhouse gas emissions are produced through the manufacture of goods and services for middle- and high-income urban consumers, providing support and incentives for people to adopt cheap, low-carbon choices can be one option. Such support will need to increase the availability of less energy-intensive housing (Reid and Satterthwaite 2007).

Global and regional networks are important for building knowledge and learning lessons. The ICLEI Local Governments for Sustainability scheme[8] has a mandate to help local governments develop action plans for urban issues, such as climate change. The ICLEI's Africa Secretariat, established in 1993, is currently running a variety of campaigns and programmes, including the Cities for Climate Protection Campaign[9] throughout the African continent, designed to work with local governments to improve urban management and address economic, environmental and social concerns. In doing so, local governments achieve the side benefits of reducing air pollution, waste and greenhouse gas emissions. One worry concerns the high priority given by international agencies to promoting mitigation, despite the fact that most African urban centres have very low levels of greenhouse gas emissions, so there is not much to mitigate. By contrast, there is a distinct lack of attention to adaptation, which is far more urgent.

Challenges

The rapid growth in urban population and size of many cities has finally forced people to recognize the shortcomings of established practices and values that dominate city planning. Over time, these have led to an accumulation of inequality, marginalization and disaster risk, especially for the poor (Pelling 2007). We know that the number of disasters in urban areas has been increasing rapidly, and most of this growth is from storms and floods, but we know too little about how urban systems respond to and shape disaster risk. There is a strong body of technical literature on infrastructure, particularly urban water, but this remains largely outside the boundaries of social science research. A clearer understanding of urban resource flows and how they will be reshaped by economic and demographic change in the context of climate change is a priority (ibid.).

Up to now, policy-makers and civil society organizations have reacted to challenges as they arise. This is no longer enough. A pre-emptive approach is needed if urbanization in developing countries is to help address social and environmental problems rather than contribute to them. In many parts of the world, an increase in the intensity and frequency of storms, rainfall and heatwaves will be so extreme that spontaneous adaptation strategies will not be sufficient. Planned adaptation initiatives, including resettlement programmes, may be necessary (Tacoli 2007). But if resettlement is needed, those who have to move need to be involved in determining where, when and how they move. For adaptation, urgent action is needed now both to address urban centres' current vulnerabilities to extreme weather, and to build in protection against likely future changes. Ninety-nine per cent of households and businesses in low-income nations do not have disaster insurance (Satterthwaite

Cities

105

et al. 2007). Yet most buildings and infrastructure have long lives; what is built now needs to be able to cope with the climate-change-induced risks over the next few decades.

There is a worry in some city administrations that a focus on trying to plan for adaptation will divert attention from broader development goals. But most of what is needed to make urban centres and urban populations more resilient to climate change is also good for development – better provision for infrastructure in informal settlements, including all-weather roads, water, sanitation and drainage, support for low-income households to enable them to build better-quality homes on safe land sites, good provision for healthcare and emergency services that also helps in disaster preparedness and post-disaster response. Planned adaptation needs competent and accountable urban governments with the capacity to make the needed investments; for most of Africa, urban governments are weak, ineffective and often unaccountable. Addressing this is, perhaps, the most difficult aspect.

The need to plan for the unexpected and develop good early warning systems that can pick up emerging crises was well demonstrated in the European heatwave of 2003, when 35,000–50,000 mainly elderly urban residents lost their lives. This was unprecedented, but not unpredictable, had lessons been learnt from earlier similar events in US cities (Pelling 2007).

There is also the issue of how to estimate the costs of adaptation for Africa's urban centres. At the moment, the figures provided by the UN Framework Convention for Climate Change for Africa represent a massive underestimate of what is needed because they take no account of the current deficits in infrastructure and services. Rather, they assume the need to climate-proof existing infrastructure, calculated on the basis of a small increment on current investments. But, to state the obvious, you cannot climate-proof infrastructure that is not there (Huq et al. 2007).

What is a climate change adaptation plan for a city?

Very few urban centres in Africa, and elsewhere, have begun to think about adaptation to climate change. In part, this is because climate change is still seen as a problem for the future. In part, it is because our knowledge of what climate change is likely to bring is at the level of larger regions, while city governments need to know what this means in practice for their city, and when they should take action. Developing a framework for adaptation will help prioritize the most urgent adaptation activities, based on understanding how climate change will impact on different sectors, and the resultant vulnerabilities. Investment can then try to avoid or limit costs, rather than react once the damage has already been done.

One of the few city governments to take adaptation seriously is Durban in South Africa,[10] building on earlier work on environmental issues, such as by the Environmental Management Department. Durban was one of the few cities in Africa to have a Local Agenda 21, in line with agreements made at the UN Earth Summit in 1992. Various departments within the municipal government have become aware of the need to factor climate change into their plans, for water supply and healthcare. But municipal officials are unlikely to act if they have little idea of what climate change means for their city. To address this, Durban's Environmental Management Department initiated the development of a Climate Protection Programme in 2004. This began by attempting to understand the global and regional climate change science, and translating this into an understanding of the implications of climate change for Durban. Key impacts include increases in temperature, changes in the distribution of rainfall (long periods of no rainfall punctuated by short periods of intense rainfall), decreased water availability, increased range of water- and vector-borne diseases, sea level rise, and the loss of biodiversity. Then a 'Headline Climate Change Adaptation Strategy' was developed to highlight how key sectors within the municipality should begin responding to unavoidable climate change. Interventions aim to enhance and expand existing initiatives (such as the modelling of vector-borne diseases and their relationship to climate change). Long-term city planning is using a model to simulate, evaluate and compare alternatives within the context of climate change, together with an assessment of the city's vulnerability in key sectors such as health, water and sanitation, coastal infrastructure, disaster management and biodiversity.

But even with a well-articulated plan and a committed government, it will always be difficult to get the needed investments in adaptation, because it is hard to demonstrate how many deaths, injuries and economic losses this will save. Funding for adaptation has to compete with funding for many other urgent issues, including improved housing conditions for large sections of the population. Adaptation needs to be seen as a key part of development to which all departments of city and municipal governments can contribute. But this is not easily achieved. And at present, the international funding for adaptation is separate from the international funding for development. Funding for adaptation is meant to address only the vulnerability and risk from climate change and not the underlying deficits in infrastructure and services that are at the core of urban centres' vulnerability to climate change (Bicknell et al. 2009: chs 2, 15, 16).

Conclusion

Climate change presents multiple hazards for those living in cities and towns in Africa. Those most at risk are the poor majority who live in squatter settlements, with weak tenure and poor access to water and sanitation. Not only are they the most vulnerable in terms of their physical situation, they also have very limited access to local government services. City municipalities tend to represent the better off, leaving informal settlements to fend for themselves. There are, however, some interesting examples of city-level plans for adaptation to climate change, from which others can learn. These aim to understand the implications of climate change for their locality, and integrate this understanding into housing, health, water and infrastructure choices. Current estimates of adaptation costs grossly underestimate the amount of money required for effective adaptation, since they assume that adaptation can be grafted on to a network of existing infrastructure which does not in fact exist.

7 | Climate change and conflict

Introduction

Climate change poses fundamental challenges for human security. The projected impacts associated with many of the scenarios outlined by the IPCC include catastrophic shifts in temperature and water supplies, as well as rising sea levels and a large increase in the incidence of hurricanes, storms and other extreme weather events. These impacts would jeopardize the security of most countries around the world, and especially low-lying small island states, which risk seeing their territory inundated. A number of observers also expect that climate change will generate a greater number and intensity of conflicts around the world. Africa has been portrayed as particularly vulnerable to such a rise in conflict, owing to its poverty, exposure to climate impacts and weak levels of state organization. But what is the evidence and analysis that might support such a view? This chapter starts by looking at links between security, conflict and climate change. It goes on to examine current patterns and causes of conflict in Africa, and assesses the likelihood of their increase as a consequence of climate change. The evidence shows that, while climate change may not cause conflict, it will increase its likelihood. It concludes by putting forward policy responses that could reduce the likelihood of increased violence stemming from climate change impacts. Such responses need to focus on shifting resources from military spending to building resilience, and investing in strong institutions for building cooperative management of scarce resources.

Security and climate change

The link between climate change and conflict can be looked at from two perspectives. From the economic perspective, the concern is that climate change will undermine development directly and reverse the economic gains of recent years. Such predicted losses stem from a fall in the volume, quality and distribution of land and water, and from direct impacts due to flood and other damage. A country's wealth and infrastructure will determine, in large part, its ability to tackle and adapt to climate change. Richer countries are better placed to invest in technology to reduce the impacts of climate change and ensure that their populations are protected and equipped with the means to adapt although, as Hurricane Katrina showed, even the USA, one of the richest nations in the world, could still suffer heavy losses in human life and economic damage. In the case of Katrina, such losses were due in part to inadequate investment in physical protection, and in part to the lack of preparedness by city and national government in terms of dealing with the needs of large numbers of poor, vulnerable people. The disruption caused by major incidents, such as a hurricane, has security implications, such as loss of control by police and army and consequent looting of property. And where investment following the incident is slow and poorly funded, this may set the scene for long-standing resentment and a sense of grievance among the people hit by the disaster.

The second perspective focuses on climate change primarily as a national and global security risk. In 2003, the US Pentagon commissioned an analysis to consider the implications of abrupt climate change for international security, and concluded that it represented the 'mother of all security problems' (Schwartz and Randall 2003). The long-term scenarios developed by the UK's Ministry of Defence list climate change among the three major drivers of global change alongside globalization and global inequality.[1] Climate extremes and uncertainty will add to existing tensions in already volatile regions of the world, such as those over rights to scarce water in the Middle East, as well as in areas such as the Arctic, where the melting of the ice cap is opening up vast new reserves of oil, gas and other minerals. Conflicts such as the war in Darfur, Sudan, seem to offer an obvious example of a region in turmoil because it has suffered drought-related problems for decades. Yet it is too simple to call Darfur 'the world's first climate

The exceptional drought and famine of 1984/85 dislocated social and economic life, killing off large numbers of animals and rendering destitute many herding and farming families. Young men from pastoral groups found themselves in the demeaning position of having to work as hired herders or wage labourers. In the dry season of 1985/86, there was large-scale raiding by Baggara tribes into southern Sudan, to seize cattle for sale in the markets of Darfur, Kordofan and Omdurman. The raids were organized by the government's military intelligence, who also supplied the weaponry. Two years later, the Janjawid militia first appeared in Darfur (originating as a coalition of Chadian militia and their Sudanese hosts), with arms supplied by Libya. Many of the men were failed nomads, their herds having died in the 1984 drought. The aftermath of famine and the influx of automatic weapons from Libya and Chad led to a large upsurge in banditry and, for many young men, their livelihoods became based around raiding and looting. At the same time, an administrative vacuum had been created in Darfur. Successive governments in Khartoum had undermined the only workable local administrative and judicial system, so that conflicts and crises were managed mainly through competing militias. What Darfur needed from the 1970s onwards was a form of governance that could manage the stresses arising from Darfurians' adaptation to their changing environment. It needed institutions to prevent and manage conflict, and ensure the effective stewardship of natural resources (Brown et al. 2007).

change war'. While it might make a good headline, the origins of conflict are far more complex than this epithet suggests (see Box 7.1 above). As de Waal notes (2007), 'In all cases, significant violent conflict erupted because of political factors, particularly the propensity of the Sudan government to respond to local problems by supporting militia groups as proxies to suppress any signs of resistance. Drought, famine and the social disruptions they brought about made it easier for the government to pursue this strategy.'

The very rapid rise in global food prices in 2007/08 generated major security concerns in countries depending heavily on food imports. Such concerns have become intertwined with worries about securing access to energy supplies, given the rapid rise in oil prices up until July 2008, the shifting geopolitics of oil and gas production, and concerns that world supplies of oil are running out. Fossil fuels have become essential for all aspects of our economic system, whether for agriculture, computing, trade or transport. The revenue generated by oil is often referred to as a 'curse' for many nations because of the damage wrought on the political and social fabric of the nation concerned, and is often at the root of civil conflict within nations. In early 2009, with food and energy prices down to five-year lows, securing supplies seems less urgent, but major importers of both food and oil are seeking to assure themselves of future access, through political and economic measures.

Why is climate change flagged as a security risk? The connection between climate change and security has been flagged up as a means to capture political attention and ensure that climate change is recognized not merely as an environmental issue, but also as a security matter. The special session of the UN Security Council in April 2007 provided a forum for governments to discuss how climate change might impact on national security. During the meeting, which was attended by representatives from over fifty countries, topics discussed included climate change, energy supply and human security. The deliberations were seen as a valuable first step in encouraging governments to take the implications of climate change for security more seriously.

Framing the climate change problem as a security risk is also a means to shift it from the desk of the minister for environment and bring it to the attention of the prime minister or president.

Campaigners for a global climate deal reckon that by making it a security matter, governments can no longer ignore the problem (Ashton 2007). Currently, budget allocations for addressing climate change, whether investing in cutting greenhouse gas emissions or in adaptation, are tiny in comparison with other elements in government expenditure. The comparison with military expenditure is particularly marked. For example, during the 2008 fiscal year, the US government budgeted $647.51 billion for military security and $7.37 billion to slow climate change, a figure that includes its support for developing countries to improve their clean energy technologies and for adaptation. In the USA, over the last five years, the ratio of military security to climate security spending has averaged 97 to 1. European spending plans are not dissimilar.[2]

In Africa, the US Pentagon, under the Trans-Sahara Counter-Terrorism Initiative (TSCTI), has provided $500 million to increase border security and counter-terrorism capacity to Mali, Chad, Niger and Mauritania. The Africa Contingency Operations Training and Assistance Program (ACOTA) has provided small arms and training for peacekeeping operations to Benin, Botswana, Côte d'Ivoire, Ethiopia, Gabon, Ghana, Kenya, Malawi, Mozambique, Nigeria, Senegal, South Africa, Uganda and Zambia.[3] Given that Africa will be one of the regions hardest hit by climate change and most in need of support for adaptation, this reliance on military spending rather than building more climate-resilient economies should be questioned.

African governments themselves also place a much higher priority on defence spending than on environmental investments, and are well represented on the list of countries with the highest military expenditure in the world, measured as a percentage of GDP. In 2006, for instance, Eritrea spent 6.3 per cent of its GDP on the military, which was the highest figure in Africa and ranked ninth in the world, and only 1.8 per cent of GDP on health. Next comes Burundi, with 5.9 per cent of its GDP going on military spending as against 0.8 per cent on health, Angola with 5.7 per cent on defence and 1.5 per cent on health and Mauritania with 5.5 per cent on defence and 2 per cent on health (CIA 2006;

UNDP 2007/08). Environmental expenditure by these governments is negligible.

Prioritizing military spending over the provision of basic services and other means to promote economic and social development is ever more ill judged, given the scale of problems that climate change will bring. A recent Oxfam report on armed conflict in Africa estimates at $300 billion the cost of conflict to the continent's development over a fifteen-year period (Oxfam 2008). According to this study, between 1990 and 2005 twenty-three African nations were involved in conflict, and on average this cost African economies $18 billion a year, a sum that equals the amount of money received in aid during the same period. For example, in Mozambique around two-thirds of dams were destroyed and 60 per cent of primary schools closed or destroyed during the decades-long war of 1970–92 (Stewart 2007).

The citation for the 2007 Nobel Peace Prize presented jointly to Al Gore and the Intergovernmental Panel on Climate Change (IPCC) recognizes their achievement in moving global warming up the political agenda, by presenting it as an existential threat.[4] 'Extensive climate changes may alter and threaten the living conditions of much of mankind. They may induce large-scale migration and lead to greater competition for the earth's resources. Such changes will place particularly heavy burdens on the world's most vulnerable countries. There may be increased danger of violent conflicts and wars, within and between states.'[5]

On accepting his Nobel Peace Prize, Al Gore called on the nations of the world to mobilize to address climate change 'with a sense of urgency and shared resolve that has previously been seen only when nations have mobilized for war'.[6] This language of struggle and preparation for the 'fight' against climate change is being used to generate energy, investment and political commitment in the face of something that could threaten human existence by making our planet 'unfit for life' (Ward and Dubos 1972). While this rhetoric may have value in forcing the comparison and helping shift budget allocations towards addressing climate change, what is the evidence that might link conflict with climate change?

Looking at conflict in Africa today

Globally, the frequency and lethality of war have been falling since the end of the cold war in 1989. But in sub-Saharan Africa, the last ten years have witnessed no such slackening of conflict, with continued very heavy loss of life in countries such as the Democratic Republic of Congo (DRC), Sudan and Angola. Since 1956, Sudan has been engulfed in civil wars that have claimed the lives of nearly two million people and have displaced 4.5 million more. Since the outbreak of fighting in DRC in August 1998, some 5.4 million people have died, while Angola has seen an estimated 500,000 people killed since 1989. A large number of refugees have been generated by these conflicts, with millions of destitute people forced into neighbouring countries.

Looking at current patterns of conflict in Africa, it is usually some combination of factors which explains the outbreak of violence. Frequently, these wars are bound up with regional politics and conflicts. For example, it is not possible to understand and resolve conflicts in Sierra Leone without looking at Côte d'Ivoire, Liberia and Guinea. Equally, the ongoing turmoil and bloodshed in DRC have been generated by a wider range of interests based in neighbouring countries keen to gain from its mineral wealth. The analysis of conflict does make clear that countries that have had a civil war in their recent past are more likely to see a resurgence of fighting than those that have lived at peace, underlining the need to avoid conflict in the first place.

Most wars are internal, happening inside states rather than between nations. They usually involve a series of warlords and armed militias supported by a range of domestic and neighbouring interests. Analysis of these conflicts has focused on two different areas of explanation, characterized by Collier (2007) as 'greed or grievance'. His analysis of civil wars over the past forty years throws light on the economic reasons underlying civil war, and the calculation of costs and gains for the leaders of a rebellion. His evidence strongly suggests that the feasibility of civil war, the revenues to be generated by control of natural resources, the availability of young men, and low levels of economic development all make conflict more likely. Greed, in his view, is a far stronger explanatory factor than grievance, the latter often being used as a justification for taking up arms, but rarely at the root of what determines whether or when civil war takes hold. This is because, according to Collier, the costs of maintaining an armed force are very considerable and rely on a steady flow of income, whether from external support, control of natural resource revenues or taxation of the population.

By contrast, Richards (2008), in describing the two civil conflicts in Sierra Leone and Côte d'Ivoire, points more to the sense of grievance felt by young men in both cases. Economic collapse, a lack of opportunities and widespread access to arms meant that they felt they had nothing to lose and much to gain from joining the rebellion, in terms of acquiring goods, status and women. In the Ivorian case, grievance had been focused on incoming migrants who had settled much of the land, whereas in Sierra Leone young men felt that the chiefs and those better off had blocked off any possibilities for escaping from misery. In both countries, the civil war was able to continue, however, because of revenues gained respectively from the sale of diamonds and other minerals, and from cocoa, in addition to funding from Libya and neighbouring states.

Does resource scarcity lead to conflict? Writers such as Homer-Dixon (2009) assert that climate change and environmental degradation will lead to major conflicts and struggle over ever scarcer resources, such as water and good land. For such writers, this tendency to resort to conflict is linked to poverty and weak institutional development, which means that there are limited means to resolve disputes. As Box 7.2 shows, however, this apparent causal link is not so clear in practice. Rather, there are often a number of factors that push people into cooperating in times of scarcity and hardship.

Looking at the current pattern of conflict in Africa, there is little solid evidence to support a direct causal link between climate change and conflict. Violent conflict arises out of a wide range of

Box 7.2 Evidence from northern Kenya

A recent study in Kenya's arid north has sought to test the links between resource scarcity and conflict, by reviewing patterns of violence between herding groups over a series of wetter and drier years (Witsenburg and Roba 2007). Marsabit mountain and the surrounding area have witnessed very rapid in-migration over the last thirty years, with many destitute herders seeking land to farm and heavy pressure from rising numbers of nomadic groups on scarce water and grazing. Automatic weapons have become far more common, bringing the risk of much more devastating damage from disputes and a higher death toll. Contrary to what might have been expected, the researchers found that conflicts were much more common in years of plenty. In wet years, when the grass was high and water could be found in many ponds scattered through the bush, it was much easier for raids to be made on the herds of others. Cattle were much fitter and could be trekked greater distances. By contrast, in dry years, the scarcity of water and the need for cooperation between different herding groups over survival strategies brought them together.

factors, none of which on its own will be a sufficient trigger for conflict (Le Billon 2007). Looking at four examples of violence from Tanzania, Kenya, Burkina Faso and Zimbabwe, Derman et al. (2007) find that 'none support the direct link between resource scarcity and violence – in each case a mixture of social inequality, lack of secure land rights, a history of conflicts and the use of land as a political reward' is responsible for conflict taking off. But they also note that 'tense and volatile situations provide opportunities for manipulation of identities', particularly where land is concerned. Most African countries currently engaged in armed conflict are characterized by poverty, inequality, weak economies, struggles over valuable resources such as oil and diamonds, and corrupt systems of justice and governance. As noted by Richards and Collier, to understand violence and conflict, a focus is needed on those 'who own resources rather than those who lack them, and those who profit from the violence rather than those who suffer from it' (Richards 2006; Collier et al. 2008: 236). This suggests that the resource curse, by exposing those in power to the temptations of great wealth, is the most powerful driver of violence and conflict.

Future flashpoints? There are several regions and trends where tensions will arise because of changes to resource availability, and where investment in better governance and institutions would help both strengthen resilience to adverse change and reduce risks of conflict.

Water management in shared river basins – As described in Chapter 3, the African continent hosts a number of major rivers shared between several nations. Yet projections for water flow over the next thirty years are worrying, given rising temperatures and changes in rainfall patterns. Combined with plans for dam building for irrigation and hydropower, the management of shared waters could generate multiple problems between states.

Data presented by Stern (2007) shows predicted water flow in the River Nile falling by 60 per cent or more over the next thirty years. This decline in river flow is based on estimated changes in rainfall in the Nile Valley catchment area, which includes countries from Uganda to Egypt. Aty Sayed (2008) argues that the large variability in projected climate scenarios over the Nile makes any policy reformulation in anticipation of climate change difficult. Instead he recommends improved water management and use, because they will benefit the region regardless of the degree and direction of rainfall change. Stronger regional cooperation would be essential to make best use of the Nile basin waters.

The Niger Basin Authority brings together nine member states, and aims to ensure coordinated management of the river basin in terms of its current and future potential, whether for energy, agriculture, transport or fisheries. As with the Nile basin, data on changes to river flow based on trends in rainfall are hard to project, given great uncertainty as regards the likely impact of global warming on West African rainfall systems. As with the Nile, however, there are plans for an accelerated programme of dam building along the river and its tributaries, which will cumulatively bring about significant cuts in water availability downstream. The extension to the Office du Niger in Mali is one such example, aiming to irrigate an additional 15,000 hectares of rice, which will require more water be taken off the river, at the expense of those downstream.

Migration of people facing crop failure – Climate change could lead many people to migrate to areas with better conditions. Some writers speak of the risk of many millions of environmental refugees being generated by drought and other changes to weather systems.[7] Experience from the droughts in West Africa and the Horn in the 1970s and 1980s shows how large numbers of people can be rendered destitute by a widespread failure of the rains, given the narrow margin of food reserves and assets available to them. The chronic drought and impoverishment of soils and farming groups in much of northern Ethiopia have generated over the past two decades a population of more than 7.5 million dependent on cash and food transfers to cover their basic needs.[8] In normal years, this large number of food-dependent people constitutes a major financial responsibility, which gets stretched beyond its limits when food prices go through the roof, as happened in 2008. In the case of Ethiopia, the government has been keen to keep impoverished rural people on the land, in their villages or camps. This is to avoid a growing landless population seeking shelter in the cities, since riots by a large and hungry urban mass can threaten and topple an unpopular government.

A major reason for land conflicts in Africa today is the large flow of people seeking land where they can settle and farm. Relations between incomers and the indigenous inhabitants are often tense, especially where there are few social and cultural values shared in common. Uncertainties regarding the rights of different groups are aggravated by the plurality of laws and systems of regulation for control over land. When land starts to become scarce, and hence valuable and marketable, such uncertainties generate fears and suspicion between neighbours, and even within families. Government interventions and establishment of agricultural projects and commercial farm enterprises can further destabilize land relations.

In the case of West Africa, the droughts of the 1970s and 1980s led to a substantial movement of people from the low-rainfall Sahel into wetter, higher-potential areas farther south. In Mali and Senegal, for example, herders moved farther south to better grazing areas and sought farmland to complement their livestock activities. Farmers also set off to find land in higher-rainfall areas, such as those from the Mossi plateau in central Burkina Faso moving to the south of the country. Many sought land in the areas under the Volta Valley Authority, where programmes to eradicate river blindness had opened up new lands for settlement along the Volta river. These incomers faced disputes and violence from indigenous people, who did not want to give up their control over lands they considered their ancestral territory. Several million farmers from Mali and Burkina Faso also travelled south to seek land in Côte d'Ivoire and Ghana. This pattern of migration to coastal countries has been of long standing, and brings in valuable income, as shown in Box 7.3. For example, Mossi migrants were positively encouraged during the colonial era as a means of providing labour for rapid expansion in coffee and cocoa farms, and migrants from Mali were welcomed in the groundnut fields of Senegal from the 1930s onwards. Such migration was further amplified after the 1970s droughts in the Sahel, with an estimated 30 per cent of the population of Côte d'Ivoire made up of people from neighbouring Burkina Faso and Mali, by the late 1990s.

The position of migrants in relation to land is complex, and has undergone a series of major changes in many parts of Africa. When land was in abundance, migrants were often sought to help populate a village and its surrounding lands, beat back the bush and keep wild animals at bay. As land has become scarcer, migrants have found that their access to land has become much more difficult. It is increasingly hard to acquire new plots of good

> ### Box 7.3 Migration brings handsome returns to households in Mali
>
> In the village of Zaradougou in southern Mali, all but two households have a plantation in Côte d'Ivoire and some have two or three holdings there. Established from the 1950s onwards, these cocoa and coffee farms have generated substantial revenues, allowing farm households in southern Mali to feed themselves and fulfil many other needs. On average, the money sent by family members working the plantation makes up one-third of total household revenue. Losing this asset and source of income would be a major blow to the viability of millions of Sahelian farmers (Brock and Coulibaly 1998).

quality, and their rights over existing plots may be contested. For example, in western areas of Ghana and Côte d'Ivoire migrants have been facing harassment and the threat of their lands being taken away from them. Land that they think they have 'bought' is considered by indigenous populations as having been on long-term loan or lease. Loans of land are transformed into rentals of shorter and shorter duration, and rental rates rise, as do demands for cash payments to avoid eviction (Lavigne-Delville et al. 2002). Such problems seem to occur particularly with a change in generation on the side either of landowner or migrant. Thus, on the death of the original landowner, his heirs may try to claim the land back. Equally, when the migrant tenant dies, his heirs may find that they must renegotiate on tougher terms for continued access to land that may have been in their hands for a generation or more.

If climate change brings about further major flows of people seeking better land elsewhere, there will need to be better ways of handling access to land, clarification of rights and managing disputes before they escalate.

Inflation in food and fuel prices – As the recent food riots in a number of African countries showed during 2008, food insecurity is another factor leading to conflict. While this bubble in food and oil prices has now been pricked, the events of 2007/08 illustrate the vulnerability of food systems in many parts of Africa to changes in supply and demand elsewhere. It is not only the rapid increase in prices but also the high level of uncertainty as regards food availability, the long queues and struggles to acquire food which generate fear and insecurity, and affect the time available to carry out other essential productive and domestic tasks.

Governments rightly fear the consequences of food shortages in their big cities, since a hungry mob constitutes a very powerful threat to their political future. The overthrow of Emperor Haile Selassie of Ethiopia was linked to the El Niño events of 1972/73, which brought droughts to the Sahel and eastern Africa. Subsequent famine and the angry response to the handling of the crisis by officials created the civil unrest that brought about the collapse of his regime (Comenetz and Caviedes 2003). Similarly, President Kountché of Niger lost power in part as a result of food shortages and riots in 1987.

Extreme events, sea level rise, disruption and damage from floods and storms – A changing climate will also bring a higher level of extreme events, such as hurricanes and storms, floods and droughts, causing damage to infrastructure, housing, energy and transport systems. Over time, sea level rise will force some people from their homes and necessitate the relocation of coastal settlements and farming areas. It is reckoned that those areas already adversely affected by weather-related hazards will experience an increase in their intensity and frequency. How will this affect conflict? It all depends on how it is managed, levels of disaster preparedness, whether it triggers a wider sense of grievance, and how far people choose to politicize such disasters.

Large-scale acquisition of land for food production – The rapid increase in food and commodity prices of 2007/08 and consequent scarcity in supply have provoked a number of countries to acquire farmland in other countries. The exact areas of land and the terms of such land acquisitions have not been published, so it is difficult to be sure of the extent of such deals. But there is a growing number of governments and companies seeking land elsewhere, particularly in Africa and Latin America, where land is considered relatively abundant and local people's property rights are frequently poorly protected. Cases cited in the press include the acquisition of a lease by South Korean company Daewoo of 1.6 million hectares of farmland in Madagascar, the settling of tens of thousands of farmers from China's Hebei Province in a number of African countries, including Angola, the leasing of 10,000 hectares by a Saudi Arabian agribusiness firm along the River Nile in the Sudan, and a 84,000-hectare farm run as a joint venture between Korean, Sudanese and Arab firms.[9]

A number of African governments are actively courting foreign investors to come and acquire land (Senegal, Nigeria, Mali, Ethiopia, Mozambique, Ghana, Tanzania), hoping thereby to transform their agricultural sector and modernize production and marketing systems. It is too early to know how such deals will work, but there are reasons for serious concern about the likely impacts on local people who had been occupying and using land now handed over to large-scale investors. It is not clear whether such modern production systems will be viable, nor how far they will offer employment and livelihoods to people displaced from their land. The past history of land-takings by governments shows land users have rarely been compensated either financially or in terms of being resettled.

In the case of Mali, the Libya Africa Investment Portfolio has signed a deal giving them control over 100,000 hectares of high-value irrigated land which will soon begin rice production destined for export to feed people in Tripoli. Concern has been expressed by farmers' organizations and NGOs for the smallholder farmers who will lose their land, as well as over the increased competition this will bring for limited supplies of irrigation water. In the case of Madagascar, the proposed land deal with Daewoo has unleashed a storm of protests, with government offices attacked and land registries burned.

These large land deals are very vulnerable, given the extensive areas they cover, which makes them impossible to police. But there may be ways to bring local people into such deals, so that they see returns from incoming investment. These could include a range of benefit-sharing schemes, such as community–corporate partnerships. There are no guarantees, however, of such deals coming about unless governments clearly understand the risks of ignoring the needs of local people and the consequences of rendering destitute and landless many farming households (Cotula et al. 2009).

Biofuel production expansion – As with large-scale land acquisitions, there are powerful interests behind a rapid expansion in biofuel production in areas deemed abundant in land, as shown in Box 7.4. The expansion in biofuels for domestic and export purposes has been one of the major consequences of climate change policy, given the targets for renewable fuels set by European, US, Chinese and other governments. Conflict over land is most likely to occur where structures of governance are weak and where local people do not have firmly documented and recognized rights over land. In many African countries, governments hold the underlying interest in land on behalf of their citizens. In such cases, it is only too easy for commercial interests to get governments to allocate them large areas of land, with little or no provision for displaced people (ibid.).

Forest carbon payments – Reducing Emissions from Deforestation and Degradation (REDD) is considered an essential part of any global deal agreed at Copenhagen at the end of 2009. In the words of Prince Charles, 'It seems to me that the central issue in this whole debate is how we put a true value on standing rainforests to the world community – we simply have to find ways of putting a price on them which makes them more valuable alive than dead.' This would involve establishing a mechanism to compensate rainforest nations and their peoples for avoiding the deforestation that they would otherwise have wished to carry out. There are multiple issues associated with such a payments mechanism, which were described earlier in Chapter 5. These include the serious risks of money being misappropriated, and forest dwellers being thrown off the land by those seeking to acquire the compensation payments. If REDD is to be a success, it is critical to find ways of avoiding such

Box 7.4 Biofuels in Mozambique

Mozambique plans a 30,000-hectare sugar-cane plantation and ethanol processing plant, known as Procana, in the district of Massingir, near the South African border. The multinational Central African Mining and Exploration Company (CAMEC), which is investing in the land and equipment, is engaged in fierce debate over water management, land rights and ethical concerns. Disputes relate to the land leased by the government to CAMEC, which international donors and community representatives said had been promised to four communities wishing to escape human–animal conflict in the Limpopo Transfrontier Park, a joint conservation initiative between Mozambique, South Africa and Zimbabwe. The second issue is one of water management, since farmers are worried that sugar-cane growing will take off most of the water available in the local river, leaving them with no possibility of developing their own irrigated agriculture (IRIN 2007).

conflicts so that REDD becomes an instrument for strengthening local livelihoods, confirming rights of occupation and use, and building more resilient systems. Without such assurances, REDD could increase the risks of conflict and impoverishment faced by those people who rely on forest land.

Looking to the future

Climate change and conflict are thus linked in multiple and complex ways. There are direct impacts from changes to water and land availability, and people will need to negotiate and adapt to the changes. There are also indirect impacts, such as those resulting from the expansion in biofuel production, and the risks associated with payments for avoided deforestation. Conflict-prone regions are not able to respond effectively to the needs of local people, as they seek to adapt to climate change. The overwhelming size of military budgets in comparison with those for social provision and environmental investments shows that lack of money is not the main problem. Rather, governments in Africa and elsewhere have been captured by interests associated with the defence industry, and see security in terms of weapons systems. The security agenda needs to be reframed to focus on the risks to human security from climate change, and the need to redesign our systems through a combination of technical, institutional and economic measures which collectively bring greater resilience. Governments in Africa need to understand the risks they face from major shifts in access to basic resources, and invest in the institutions that can broker cooperation between competing interests.

> From everything that we know about how mutually interlocking factors such as poverty, bad governance and the legacy of past conflicts generate risks of new violence, it is safe to predict that the consequences of climate change will combine with other factors to put additional strain on already fragile social and political systems ... These are the conditions in which conflicts flourish and cannot be resolved without violence because governments are arbitrary, inept and corrupt. (Smith and Vivekananda 2007)

8 | Africa and the low-carbon economy

Introduction

The world is increasingly interconnected and changing very rapidly, as has been evident over 2008/09, given the impacts around the world stemming from the credit crunch, the collapse of many financial institutions, and subsequent economic recession. The globalization of markets, finance and information brings opportunities as well as risks. The changing perception of biofuels is a good example of how rapidly the policy choices made in Brussels, Beijing and Washington can impact on the rest of the world. As described below, from a largely positive assessment of their merits in 2006, biofuels became the whipping boy of many environmentalists two years later. Given the rapidity of change, and the speed with which new policy initiatives are being generated, African countries risk missing out on the economic gains to be made from changing market conditions. The growth in carbon finance is one such opportunity for earning revenue. Risks include growing concern among consumers in rich countries about reducing their carbon footprint and, hence, cutbacks in spending on air-freighted fruit and vegetables from Kenya, Tanzania and Zambia. Doing well in global markets requires a mix of entrepreneurial activity and an understanding of the policy processes that establish and open up new markets and products. African countries need to be closely linked to the design and management of new global policy-making to ensure they can access emerging markets.

This chapter describes a set of major opportunities facing African nations today, linked to climate change and associated policy responses. These include those linked directly to measures aimed at cutting greenhouse gas emissions, such as carbon pricing, and more indirect consequences from climate-related policy, such as changes in demand for oil, and shifts in tourism and travel. As with so many areas of international decision-making, the interests and perspectives of African nations and their peoples are rarely taken into account when global leaders get around the table. If African people and their economies are to profit from a future low-carbon economy, their leaders must make their voices heard more loudly in current debates. Otherwise, new markets and institutions will be set up which respond to the needs of rich and middle-income countries rather than poorer, more vulnerable states.

Access to carbon markets

The agreement to cut greenhouse gas emissions under the Kyoto protocol has led to the establishment of a market for carbon emission reductions, often referred to as the 'carbon market'. In fact, it is not carbon as such which is traded, but rather reductions in carbon emissions. Examples of carbon trading systems include the EU's Emission Trading System, the Clean Development Mechanism (CDM), cap and trade systems in a number of US states, and voluntary carbon trading enterprises. These markets for carbon emission reductions offer an important and growing potential source of finance for Africa's development.

Carbon prices have fluctuated considerably given parallel fluctuations in the political commitment at global level to agreeing further cuts in emissions. Following the climate summit in Poznań in December 2008, however, and the election of Barack Obama as US president, there is likely to be a tougher regime of emission cuts agreed as a central part of the post-Kyoto treaty. This means that the longer-term future of the carbon market looks bright. Given scientific evidence of the need for ever greater and more urgent cuts in carbon emissions, the price of carbon can be expected to rise, from its average for early 2009 on the EU's ETS of $12–18 per ton of carbon emissions reduced, to $65–100 per ton in 2020. The International Energy Agency (IEA) reckons, however, that a price of $200 per ton is needed to bring about sufficient cuts to meet the 2050 goal of halving global emissions from the levels in 1990.

The CDM is one means to gain access to carbon finance. But

many developing countries interested in participating find that the procedures are complex. CDM benefits to date have largely bypassed Africa, in large part because of the low level of emissions. The high transaction costs of accessing CDM finance have also been a major hurdle.

Voluntary carbon markets

Growing interest and concern among individuals and companies as regards reducing their carbon footprint have generated a lively, rapidly growing voluntary carbon market. It is voluntary in the sense that neither individuals nor the companies have a legal obligation, as yet, to demonstrate cuts in emissions, though the establishment of individual carbon allowances would change this. Carbon offsets have become popular as a means to neutralize a particular activity, such as air travel, or holding a major conference. A recent survey found more than sixty companies offering carbon offsets for sale

---

Box 8.1 AdMit – a novel approach to carbon offsets

AdMit is a new alternative to carbon offsetting that addresses many of the weaknesses of voluntary carbon trading. AdMit guarantees a payment directly from polluters to some of the world's poorest communities which are most vulnerable to climate change. So it channels resources to those who need it most. It avoids focusing only on the carbon offset requirements and combines this with building adaptive capacity.

With AdMit, people who want to offset their carbon emissions can buy into a project that has clear benefits in terms of adaptation to climate change. It involves a partnership between people in an area vulnerable to climate change and consumers eager to reduce the damage their emissions have been causing. Such projects include a range of initiatives in urban and rural areas which combine greater resilience in livelihood systems and shelter with improved management of carbon above and below ground (IIED 2009).

Africa and the low-carbon economy

---

on the voluntary market. While many African countries have limited scope for selling emission reductions from industrial activities, there are multiple opportunities for sequestering carbon through changes in land management. The voluntary market is much easier to access than the CDM, because the procedures and systems for verification are much less stringent. While this brings the risks of fraud and misselling, it also makes it much easier for small-scale carbon projects to find a buyer. There are a number of uncertainties surrounding how to measure and verify the amounts of carbon being sequestered through changes in land management. But this situation could change with better understanding of the carbon cycle in land-based ecosystems and suitable verification schemes. Many African nations could then take part in global efforts to slow the rate of increase in atmospheric CO_2, and benefit from the associated financial and technological transfers (Williams et al. 2007).

Avoided deforestation and land use changes

Africa might benefit substantially from the proposed payments mechanism to encourage avoided deforestation – known as Reduced Emissions from Deforestation and Degradation (REDD). The principle here is that countries controlling their deforestation and thereby reducing GHG emissions associated with clearing land can receive compensation from a global fund. The payment per hectare would need to be sufficient to offset the incentive to deforest and put the land under soy and palm oil. Such a fund is likely to be agreed as part of the post-Kyoto treaty, though the details of its operations are yet to be determined. Uncertainties also exist concerning how avoided deforestation will be measured and monitored, and who within these countries will receive the compensation. The main countries in Africa with large areas of tropical forest are those in the Congo basin, such as the Democratic Republic of Congo (DRC). Currently, there is no confidence among carbon buyers that the DRC, or many other African countries, can demonstrate a system of property rights and good governance that would satisfy the market. Consequently, considerable investment will be needed to make such countries ready for REDD.

Attention is also now focusing on non-forest systems to assess their potential role in sequestering carbon. These include grasslands, where it is estimated that each hectare can store from 2 to 9 tons of carbon per hectare each year if land and vegetation are managed more intensively (Tennigkeit and Wilkes 2008), and agroforestry parklands of the Sahel, where 20–40 tons of carbon per hectare can be stored in a mix of indigenous trees and shrubs. Although these figures are much less than the estimates for tropical forest areas, they represent a significant source of new revenue for the inhabitants of these regions.

Energy options

Ensuring access to clean and efficient energy would greatly increase the options for economic growth and diversification in Africa. At present, about 1.6 billion people worldwide lack access to electricity and about 2.5 billion rely on wood and charcoal as their primary source of energy. A significant proportion of these people are found in sub-Saharan Africa, where only 25 per cent of people have access to electricity. The rapid rise in oil prices over 2007/08 hit fuel-importing countries very hard, particularly in the transport and power sectors, making it ever more valuable to identify new options for clean energy. Renewable energy technologies, given their environmental advantages over conventional energy sources, their suitability for use in rural areas and their potential for local income-generating activities, present a good opportunity to break with conventional patterns of energy development, such as centralized generating systems, which have failed so far to meet the needs of the poor.

Promising options include a range of new solar and photovoltaic systems, small-scale biofuel production and processing, increased energy efficiency, wind and water power. Investment in new technology would benefit from better access to funding, including bilateral and multilateral assistance, carbon financing and concessionary lending. Strategies being pursued by funders, such as the Global Village Energy Partnership (GVEP), include small-scale business development to train 'energy entrepreneurs',

Africa and the low-carbon economy

policy and regulatory reforms, capacity building and training. There is a growing network of organizations and partnerships supporting renewable energy in Africa, which has the potential for galvanizing much new village-based activity, as well as providing lighting for schools and clinics.

Biofuels

There are two main forms of biofuel: bioethanol derived from cellulose-rich crops, such as sugar cane and maize, and biodiesel, which is made from oil seeds, such as jatropha (*Jatropha curcas*, a member of the euphorbia family) and palm oil. Currently the world market is dominated by bioethanol, with global production of 40 million litres, of which Brazil and the USA are the main producers (World Bank 2007). By contrast, biodiesel currently constitutes only one-sixth of total volume.

There are several reasons for the growth of biofuels production. The first is the potential to save significant amounts of carbon, while maintaining current transport systems based on the internal combustion engine. But not all biofuel production systems do actually save carbon, given high levels of carbon embodied in mechanization and fuels used in the cultivation, processing and transport of biofuels prior to their distribution. Ethanol derived from maize in the USA is reckoned to require more carbon-based inputs per litre than it saves. Second is the desire for national energy security, given uncertainty regarding future energy supplies and the need to reduce the energy import bill. The recent slump in oil prices has reduced somewhat the urgency felt by oil-importing countries to achieve greater energy independence. Equally, many biofuel production systems cannot compete with oil at less than $40 per barrel. Oil prices will start going back up once the current economic downturn has passed. Third, biofuels generate a new demand for agricultural products, reducing commodity surpluses and improving commodity prices. Hence, they are seen as offering a means to diversify the farm economy and generate higher rural incomes.

The market in biofuels is driven very largely by government pol-

Box 8.2 Biofuels in Nigeria and Mozambique

Several African countries have biofuel research projects under way. One of them, Nigeria, the world's largest producer of cassava, currently uses a 10 per cent blending standard of cassava ethanol with gasoline, and is keen to develop cassava as an alternative to fossil fuel. Nigeria's aim is to produce cassava ethanol worth over US$150 million every year, once it establishes a suitable infrastructure. This includes construction of fifteen ethanol plants with assistance from Brazil. In May 2007, the government announced plans to establish a US$100 million 'biofuel town' near the capital, Lagos. This will create a 600-hectare settlement of 1,000 bioenergy experts. Nigeria also aims to start importing Brazilian ethanol-powered vehicles by 2010.

Mozambique has developed an effective biofuel sector based on sorghum and sugar cane, and the government has set aside over US$700 million for biofuel research, production and promotion. Energy experts say Mozambique has the potential to be a 'biofuel superpower'. Sufficient rainfall allows for extensive production of sugar cane, which is currently the most efficient crop for ethanol in terms of production cost. Scientists from the International Crops Research Institute for the Semi-Arid Tropics (ICRISAT) are also developing for Mozambique sorghum varieties and hybrids that have higher amounts of sugar-rich juice in their stalks (Chege 2007).

icy. The EU, for example, has proposed a mandatory target by 2020 for 10 per cent of all member states' transport fuels to come from biofuels, and similar targets have been set by the USA, Brazil, India and China. As a result global demand is expected to increase by around 20 per cent per year up to 2011, reaching 92 million metric tons. The expected mismatch between global demand and supply within these regions means that international trade in biofuels is expected to grow very rapidly in the coming years. African countries have a very limited market share in biofuel production and trade at present, but there has been great interest from governments and investors seeking to establish an industry in a number of countries. One reason is the prospect of attracting investment, for example through accessing some funds from carbon trading systems (e.g. the Clean Development Mechanism). Another is that many developing countries located in tropical and subtropical areas have, or may develop, a comparative advantage for feedstock production, such as sugar cane and oil palm (Oxfam 2007; Dufey et al. 2007). This creates an opportunity for African nations to develop a new export market for their agricultural produce and to increase export revenues. Biofuel production could potentially improve agricultural employment, incomes and livelihoods, especially when cultivation involves small-scale farmers. Box 8.2 describes the biofuel expansion taking place in Nigeria and Mozambique.

Where will biofuels be grown?

The African continent has been presented by some as containing large tracts of 'idle' land, available for allocation to biofuel production. For example, the government of Mozambique has stated that only 9 per cent of the country's arable land is currently in use and that there are therefore more than forty million hectares available for allocation. But often people rely on this land for cultivation, grazing and gathering wild food. The fact that biofuels will make agriculture more profitable will lead to an increase in land value, and this will inevitably put pressure on land access for poorer, less powerful groups, many of whom risk losing their land. The tenure status of these lands is also complex and often based on customary rights, with no written contracts, which makes it easier for governments and investors to ignore local user rights.

In Tanzania, for example, an area in the Wami basin has been hallmarked for production of sugar cane as a biofuel feedstock, but is currently occupied by thousands of small-scale rice farmers, who face eviction as a result (African Biodiversity Network 2007). This creates an urgent need to develop local consultation, arbitration and proper compensation to protect the rights of poor people in the land allocation process. Although large-scale systems are often favoured as the ideal model for biofuel production, there may be models based on small-scale farmers which can work as effectively. For example, in Mali the government is promoting small-scale production of jatropha to meet local energy needs, such as rural electricity for pumps, lighting and mills, and access to land for biofuel cultivation is based on agreements with local villagers.

The future scale and direction of biofuel use are subject to rapid development in production and processing technology. For many developing countries it would make sense to wait for the emergence of second-generation technologies, 'leapfrogging' to these technologies in the next few years (von Braun 2007). These second-generation biofuels are derived from woody matter, which would make them less competitive with food crop production.

Since late 2007, there have been growing concerns about the impact of biofuel production on food prices, given the tripling of world market prices for rice, maize and wheat. For rural households that are net producers of food, higher prices for agricultural commodities should bring gains in welfare. But many rural households in Africa are actually net buyers of food, for whom higher prices have an adverse impact. This has led EU governments to reassess the targets set, and look to certification of biofuel production to provide greater assurance that these crops are being grown in accordance with certain social and environmental standards. There are large differences in the water requirements of different biofuel crops; for example, sugar cane requires 4,000 litres of water to produce 1 litre of ethanol, compared to sweet sorghum, which requires 1.3 litres of water per biofuel litre (ICRISAT 2008). Thus, choice of which biofuel crop to invest in needs to be considered in the light of future competition for water, given the expected impacts of climate change.

Africa and 'peak oil'

The high price of oil over recent years, and anxiety regarding longer-term supplies, has led to extensive exploration for new oil reserves, both offshore and in the interior. At present, the principal oil and gas producers in Africa are Angola, Nigeria, Libya and Sudan, but recently new finds have been made in Saõ Tomé, Ghana and Mauritania. Western countries are keen to diversify away from their reliance on Middle Eastern sources of oil, and, for example, within the next decade, 25–35 per cent of US imports could come from oil reserves located in the Gulf of Guinea. Oil provides a major source of government revenue, but the economic benefits are often offset by lack of transparency, high levels of corruption and conflict. It is for this reason that such fossil-fuel riches are often termed the natural resource 'curse'.

Interest from the USA, China and India in Africa's relatively new status as an oil exporter makes ever more complex Africa's political positioning in the climate change negotiations. While governments and the elite are likely to gain riches from the exploitation of fossil fuels, the poor majority will suffer ever greater adverse effects of global warming. Looking forward over the next twenty years, it is unclear how the price of oil will be affected by a tighter cap on GHG emissions, and a rising price of carbon. In the absence of technology that can capture and store carbon emissions from the burning of oil and gas, one should expect the price of oil and gas to fall, since the costs of burning it will rise.

Many African countries are highly dependent on oil for transport, given very limited railway infrastructure. Landlocked countries such as Mali, Burkina Faso and Niger were particularly hard hit by price rises over the period 2005–08. The price of diesel in Zambia, for example, rose from $1 to about $2.80 per litre over the twelve months to June 2008, adding to the costs of using machines such as irrigation pumps. Fertilizer, which is especially energy intensive to produce and transport, rose from US$30 a 50-kilogram bag in December 2007 to $70 in August 2008. Fertilizer subsidies were common in the 1960s and 1970s, but two decades of structural adjustment have ensured that by 2000 very few farmers could afford to purchase more than a tiny amount. Fertilizer remains substantially more expensive than in rich and middle-income countries, which explains why African farmers use one-tenth of the global average per hectare.

Over the next twenty or thirty years, agricultural production systems face serious challenges if they are to maintain the productivity of soils, and in the face of climate change. For some observers, organic agriculture seems to be the answer, by reducing demand for carbon-intensive inputs of chemicals, and increasing levels of organic matter in the soil. In many regions, organic farming may provide a significant option for food production, but there are also many farming systems in which high population density and long occupation of the land mean that soils have become very poor in nutrients and organic matter, and it would take many years to rebuild their content and structure. Consequently, a review of fertilizer subsidies is now under way, with countries like Malawi reinstating them as they recognize the multiple benefits generated for the agricultural sector.

Food miles, carbon and climate

Consumer concerns over carbon 'footprints' have led many people to question the sustainability of air-freighted fresh fruit and vegetables, which are too perishable to be transported by sea. African countries, such as Kenya, Zambia and Tanzania, gain considerable revenue from air-freighted exports to Europe. UK consumers spend over £1 million every day on produce from sub-Saharan African countries and 87 per cent of UK green bean imports are from five African countries (MacGregor and Vorley 2006). The total supply chain linking African farmers to consumption of fresh fruit and vegetables in the UK is estimated to provide a livelihood to 1–1.5 million people (Garside et al. 2007).

Given the ever-increasing influence of climate change on buying behaviour and legislation, and the future resource constraints caused by peak oil, the long-term viability of a business model reliant on air freight has been questioned. This is reflected by the proposal by the UK's Soil Association to withdraw its organic certificate from air-freighted fruit and vegetables. This would strike a blow to Africa's organic farmers, who receive higher revenues from organic produce than from conventional farming. An analysis of carbon emissions associated with all parts of the food chain, however,

---

Box 8.3   Food miles – carbon footprint of food choices

- Driving six and a half miles to buy your shopping emits more carbon than flying a pack of Kenyan green beans to the UK.
- Air freighting fruit and vegetables from Africa accounts for less than one-tenth of 1 per cent of the UK's greenhouse gas emissions.
- Emissions produced by growing flowers in Kenya and flying them to the UK can be less than a fifth of those grown in heated and lighted greenhouses in Holland.

  Source: www.dfid.gov.uk

---

including crop production, processing and distribution, as well as transport, showed that the amounts of carbon associated with air freight were minor in comparison with, say, the carbon embodied in chemical fertilizer, the heating of greenhouses or food distribution between supermarket centres. The concern over food miles shows the risk of people focusing on a single part of the food chain, rather than looking at the bigger picture (see Box 8.3).

Rights to ecological space

A fairer way to address 'food miles' is by considering the amount of 'ecological space' to which every citizen of the world is entitled. Taking the overall capacity of the global atmosphere to absorb greenhouse gases, the per capita right to emit carbon dioxide can be calculated as approximately 2 tons of CO_2 per year. In the UK, the annual carbon dioxide (CO_2) emissions per person are currently 9.2 tons, by comparison with per capita emissions in Kenya of 0.2 tons and in Uganda of 0.1 tons. Thus, currently, sub-Saharan African countries have considerable reserves of ecological space compared with the countries to which they export.

Consumers, policy-makers and food chain businesses should base decisions on good information. If environmental harm is to be weighed against developmental gains, it is essential to consider the full context, so that the degree of environmental harm is put into the context of Africa's current very limited use of 'ecological space' (DfID 2007). Otherwise, consumers in the UK run the risk of 'saving the planet' at someone else's expense.

Tourism, travel and climate change

The global tourism sector is large and continues to grow rapidly from 800 million tourists in 2005 to 842 million in 2007. Africa's share of the global market remains small, at less than 4 per cent of the total, but it is nevertheless significant for a number of countries and has grown very fast. In Gambia, tourism is the second-highest earner of foreign revenue, with benefits to local employment in a range of sectors. Tourism also provides more than 22 per cent of foreign export earnings for countries like Morocco, Egypt and Mauritius (ODI 2006). The same is true for Tanzania, as shown in Box 8.4. Climate change will, however, bring changes to the tourist economy. Many countries on the tourist trail already have very variable climates. Rising temperatures and water shortages will make them less appealing destinations. The distribution of wildlife will alter as a result of increased drought and changed temperatures, causing disruption to Africa's system of game parks and protected areas.

The effects of climate change on tourism will not be uniform, with current sunshine destinations, such as the Mediterranean, North Africa and South Africa, all losing out.[1] Global warming is likely to bring about a restructuring of tourism, with people seeking cooler regions, away from sun and sand on the coast to inland and higher-altitude areas. Since few parts of the African continent are cool, global warming will not be good for the tourism sector, nor for the associated income-generating activities, such as farmers growing crops for the hotel trade, handicraft industries and local businesses that service the visitors. Shifts in consumer preference, the global economic downturn and concerns about air travel and carbon footprints will further reduce the tourist sector in many countries (Viner and Agnew 1999).

Box 8.4 Tanzania's tourism

Tanzania is simultaneously one of the most economically poor and biologically rich countries in Africa. Income from tourism has grown from US$6 million in 1990 to US$725 million in 2001. Since then the figures have grown even more, with 719,030 tourists visiting the country in 2007, generating US$1 billion in revenue and making tourism the leading foreign exchange earner. Hopes are that there will be a further increase in 2008. The president of Tanzania calls tourism a key weapon in 'a heightened onslaught on poverty' (URT 2002), and the country's Rural Development Strategy states that a 'pro-poor tourism strategy will aim to unlock opportunities for economic gains and other livelihood benefits' (ibid.; URT 2001).

China and Africa

China has become a major influence on the economics and politics of many African countries, as a source of investment and aid, a major trading partner buying raw materials in exchange for manufactured goods, and able to provide access to research and technology. The rapid rise in China's influence can be seen in the annual growth in trade between China and Africa of more than 30 per cent annually since 2000. This influence is likely only to accelerate, given the geopolitical shifts under way globally, which are bringing about a relative decline of Europe and North America, in relation to the other G20 nations.

China's role in Africa has often been portrayed as damaging, and focused only on extracting oil, minerals, timber and other resources, but paying no heed to corruption and conflict. A different perspective, however, would emphasize the major investments made by the Chinese in roads and railways, and the lack of interference in the politics and governance of African countries (Alden 2007). China can potentially bring much-valued agricultural research and technology, of greater relevance to African smallholders than the high science of Europe and North America. Whether these benefits will reach the majority of Africans depends on how clearly they can make their own voices heard. Currently, many governments are more interested in advancing their own interests at the expense of the poor majority, often with the funds of the international donor community (Moyo 2009). The Chinese influence in Africa has also become a much more diffuse set of relationships, only some of which are in the power of China's government to manage. An increasing number of entrepreneurs, traders and farmers are getting involved in Africa in ways that escape attempts by both the Chinese and host governments to frame and control their activities.

A voice in international decision-making

In 2007, sub-Saharan Africa's share of the global economy was slightly below 1 per cent, a position it has maintained for a couple of decades. This weak global economic status has its parallel in global politics and rule-making, with the consequence that African governments have had to live with and make the best of rules and organizations designed by other, more powerful countries and regions, such as the USA and EU. Thus, as was seen earlier, the design of the Clean Development Mechanism has not favoured access to this source of funding for the diverse and smaller-scale needs of many African countries.

With negotiations under way for the next climate change agreement, there is every likelihood that the particular needs and priorities of African nations will again be ignored in the rush to finalize a text to which the big polluting countries can sign up. African countries form part of the 'Group of 77' during the UNFCCC talks, but this single grouping masks a very diverse set of powers and interests, since it includes the very poorest countries alongside OPEC nations, China, India and Brazil. Africa does not negotiate as a single bloc, unlike the small island nations, which operate as the Association of Small Island States (AOSIS) and act as an effective voice for the interests of those nations most at risk from sea level rise. Yet African nations stand to lose a great deal from climate change, being hard hit by many adverse impacts and gaining few, if any, positive benefits, unlike Canada and Russia. Rapid, ambitious and effective cuts in greenhouse gas emissions are critical for Africa's future.

But the rules for the next climate agreement will be written by the most powerful groups, unless a strong, clear set of perspectives is voiced by those groups with most to lose. There is therefore an urgent need to strengthen the ability of African governments and their citizens to understand and engage with the climate change debate. This requires work at the level of the African Union in developing a continent-wide strategy, and at the level of particularly vulnerable countries. This will require a mix of activities, such as strengthening negotiating capacity, tactics and strategy; developing input from research, civil society and community groups; assessing the costs of climate change for different countries; and testing out practical options for adaptation. It should also include programmes of public information to generate understanding among the population of the challenges to be faced.

Strengthening the adaptation process

There are many important interventions for strengthening adaptation to climate change in Africa. Some of these are immediate, as outlined in the National Adaptation Programmes of Action (NAPAs). Others require longer-term investment in infrastructure for disaster risk reduction, clean energy and better water management. Most governments in Africa have only recently started paying serious attention to adaptation and the impacts of climate change. For many it is still seen as an environmental problem of principal interest to Western nations, rather than something that will have major consequences for their own economies and societies.

If African people are to gain from a future 'low-carbon economy', their governments must play a more effective role in designing the post-2012 agreement in ways that match the development aspirations of the majority. This means findings ways to reduce the vulnerability of millions of urban dwellers, farmers and herders to climatic events, such as floods and erratic rainfall. It also means seizing opportunities opening up from new carbon finance for funding adaptation and clean energy schemes. If farmers, forest people and squatters are to construct a more resilient future, they will need, above all, for government to recognize and support their rights to manage and control the land, water, forests and shelter on which they depend. The current emphasis on cutting carbon – whether with avoided deforestation schemes, pushing biofuel cultivation at the expense of food crops, or cutting back on air-freighted vegetables – risks pushing all the costs of cutting carbon emissions on to poor people in Africa, who have neither the voice nor the power to design the world in ways that would bring greater benefits to themselves and their families.

Looking forward: Africa and the global economy

African countries are hugely diverse in terms of their size, re-sources and ability to exploit new economic opportunities. For example, the proposed payment of compensation for reduced deforestation is currently focused on tropical moist forestlands, such as those found in the Congo basin and parts of coastal West Africa. Dryland nations in southern Africa and the Sahel will not benefit from carbon finance unless new products can be designed which offer a verifiable carbon sink in the soils and woodlands of the savannahs. Countries also vary greatly in their reliance on sectors such as oil and mining, tourism and biofuel potential, and thus will find their interests affected in diverse ways, depending on how demand for these goods and services shifts. Africa as a continent finds it hard to speak with one voice, because of this diverse set of interests and needs. Equally, African leaders are rarely brought to the top table when big global negotiations are being hammered out, with South Africa and Nigeria the rare exceptions. This inability of African leaders to get their voices heard in the corridors of power finds a parallel in the weak ability of many citizens to hold their own governments to account.

The current economic downturn has highlighted again the vulnerability of many poorer countries in Africa and elsewhere, faced with a fall in remittances from migrants overseas, a decline in foreign investment, a collapse in the price of many export commodities and a tightening of trade credit. African governments yet again find themselves at the end of the line, given the prior importance of bailing out Western banks over shoring up basic social and environmental infrastructure in poorer nations. There remains a shocking gap in the readiness with which cash can be found from the UK's and other treasuries to plug holes in banks and building societies that affect the lives of voters in the West and the meanness associated with finding funds for addressing crises that strike less close to home. We live in an increasingly interconnected world, but our habits and political structures remain compartmentalized. It is a worrying mismatch as we head into the risky and uncertain territory of climate change.

9 | Looking forward

Global emissions of greenhouse gases are rising ever more rapidly, and considerably faster than in the models used by the IPCC. The ice at the poles has been melting much faster than expected, with the Arctic ice cap shrinking to its smallest size in the summers of 2007 and 2008. Temperatures and sea levels have been rising at the top end of the model predictions, suggesting that the latest report by the IPCC, issued in 2007, presents a conservative interpretation of our current and likely future situation. At present rates of growth, in the next five years we shall pass the point at which greenhouse gases have reached 450 parts per million of CO_2 equivalent, which means we are set for a 50 per cent chance of global mean temperatures rising by at least 2°C. Scientists such as Bob Watson argue that 'there is no doubt that we should aim to limit changes in the global mean surface temperature to 2°C above pre-industrial, but given this is an ambitious target, and we don't know in detail how to limit greenhouse gas emissions to realise a 2 degree target, we should be prepared to adapt to 4°C'.[1]

Most scientists and policy analysts agree that we must reach peak global emissions by 2015, and achieve a rapid decrease from then onwards, so that by 2050 we will have cut total emissions by 50–80 per cent in comparison with 1990 levels. For rich countries, which have been primarily responsible for the stock of greenhouse gases in the atmosphere, this will mean a cut of more than 80 per cent by 2050. To attain this level will mean reductions of 25–40 per cent by 2020 for countries in Europe, North America and Japan, and the adoption of targets by middle income countries, such as China, to cut back on their large and rapidly growing emissions. Scientist James Hansen says these reductions will not be enough, and that we should seek to take carbon out of the atmosphere so we can return to a situation where there are 350 parts per million (ppm) of CO_2 equivalent in the atmosphere. This would give greater security against crossing tipping points, as well as reducing risks to more vulnerable countries, such as small island states.

Simple mathematics shows us the scale of the cuts required, to move towards a more sustainable relationship between humankind and the global atmosphere (Stern 2009). In 1990, the world emitted around 40 Gigatonnes (Gt) of greenhouse gases, while today this has risen to more than 50 Gt per year. If we are to reduce emissions to 50 per cent of the 1990 level by 2050, this is equivalent to a global total of 20 Gt. Given a likely world population of some nine billion people in 2050, this will mean that, on an equitable basis, each person can emit no more than 2 tons per person. This contrasts with current levels of 10–12 tons per person in Japan and the EU, more than 20 tons per person in the USA and Canada, more than 5 tons per person in China and approximately 1 ton per person in India. By contrast, emission levels in sub-Saharan Africa are around 0.7 tons per person. If we are to construct a fairer and more equitable world, it is clear where the major cuts must fall.

Nevertheless, the scale of the challenge is daunting. We need to shift to a global economy in which carbon is largely eliminated from our economic system. But, for the last 100 years or more, we have relied ever more heavily on fossil fuels for providing the essentials of life, whether they be electricity, power for transport, energy for making fertilizer and processing minerals, or the wide range of oil-derivative products that are ever-present in daily life, such as plastics. It will take a concerted global effort to set the ambition high enough and carry this through into the policies, regulations and incentives required to achieve such a transformation of the economy. At the time of writing, while there are some signs of hope, such as the understanding and commitment of the new Obama administration in the USA to address climate change, there are great uncertainties about the extent to which political leaders in the major emitting countries feel the need to take bold steps. The global recession has made many politicians and publics feel nervous of further change, just at a time when confident, ambitious steps are most needed.

The contours and success of a global climate deal will depend in large part on relations between China and the USA, and the extent to which each decides to pursue the strategic goal of designing the new technologies and policies that will provide the foundation for a low-carbon economy in future. Both countries have launched major fiscal stimulus packages, in which low-carbon energy and investment in public transport infrastructure are significant components. Most observers of the climate change negotiations accept that the agreement reached at the Copenhagen summit will be a set of high-level principles with much of the detail to be worked out in subsequent sessions. Thus, getting agreement on the higher-level elements will depend on the USA and China identifying clearly their future gains from moving towards a low-carbon economy, and finding ways of paying off the losers, such as those reliant on coal, oil and gas.

Where does Africa sit within this negotiation process? As described earlier, Africa as a continent has been a very minor contributor to global greenhouse gases, yet will bear many of the adverse consequences. The previous chapters have outlined expected impacts in the fields of water, food production, forests and cities, as well as the risks that climate change will bring in terms of generating conflict over scarce resources. African countries are particularly vulnerable, owing in part to their reliance on land, agriculture and natural resources, and in part to high levels of poverty and poor governance. In many areas, climate change impacts will further exacerbate poverty and render more taxing achievement of the Millennium Development Goals. It is also evident, however, that the impacts of climate change are quite diverse. While many areas will become hotter and drier, a few regions may gain increased rainfall, at least in the short to medium term. Making best use of rainfall and other water resources will be key to successful adaptation, at the level of the field, village, watershed and river basin.

The climate negotiations are focused around two main strands; first ensuring the necessary cuts in greenhouse gases are made, known as mitigation, and second, addressing the need for adaptation to the impacts that are now inevitable, owing to the slowness of our global response. Also subject to negotiation are the financial and technology transfers necessary to enable both mitigation and adaptation. Stern estimates we need to invest the equivalent of 2 per cent of global GDP to achieve the cuts in greenhouse gases needed to stay below 500 ppm. In 2008, global GDP was estimated to be $69 trillion, so that 2 per cent would provide $1,380 billion. A more ambitious target, such as 450 ppm, would be more expensive. A figure of 2 per cent is small in relation to the amounts of money many people spend on insurance to protect their house, health and car. And it should be remembered that the costs of inaction will rapidly escalate to the point where it may be impossible to avoid catastrophic impacts from climate change.

Adaptation costs have also been estimated, though clearly these also depend on the assumptions made regarding the scale of impacts and the degree of adaptation that can be achieved. A wide range of estimates of adaptation costs have been produced by the World Bank, UNDP and Oxfam, ranging from $4 billion to $109 billion a year. The latest report from the UN Framework Convention on Climate Change now suggests that total adaptation costs could rise by 2030 to between $41 and $171 billion per year, by far the largest part being infrastructure investment. Comparing the relative costs of mitigation and adaptation would suggest that mitigation is a lot more expensive than adaptation. This could lead people into thinking that we can afford to wait before making cuts in greenhouse gases, as costs of adaptation are less than one-tenth those of mitigation. There is increasing concern, however, that the ballpark figures on adaptation that have currency today may be gross underestimates by a factor of at least five, and in some areas ten.[2] This underestimation is the consequence of the methods by which these figures have been generated. There are also increasing worries that the pace of climate change is considerably faster than had been predicted, which means that impacts will be greater and more immediate. Additionally, the debate on adaptation assumes that we can actually adapt to different impacts. In practice, it may be almost impossible for human and ecological systems to adjust to more extreme changes in rainfall, temperature and sea level rise.

In practice, many impacts may be very difficult to accommodate, even through expenditure of large sums of money.

The current approach to adaptation has been to assess potential costs, design adaptation plans at national and other levels, establish a global funding mechanism, and identify sources of revenue to cover the estimated costs. This follows a similar path to that followed by previous attempts to tackle global problems, such as Agenda21, which stemmed from the Rio Earth Summit in 1992, meeting the Millennium Development Goals by 2015, and a range of action plans aimed at combating desertification, addressing tropical deforestation and stemming the loss in biodiversity. While making plans and setting targets would seem the obvious first steps to addressing a big problem, we should recognize the limited success of such approaches to date, and see how best to bridge the gap between plans and making real progress on the ground.

There are several clear areas of weakness. First, the making of a plan often seems to substitute for action. Second, governments need to recognize the limited role that they can play in effecting many of the changes sought and should focus on setting the policy, regulatory and legal framework to provide strong incentives for people to change behaviour, establishing the funding mechanism, and encouraging a decentralized, tailored approach. Third, a stronger grasp of political economy is required in design and monitoring of plans, given the range of interest groups that may seek to block progress. Fourth, it should be remembered that governments need both policies and administrative capacity. Often government policy ambitions very greatly exceed practical ability to deliver on the ground, particularly in poor countries.

A stronger voice for Africa in global arenas

The African continent faces difficulties in getting its voice heard in global arenas. The combination of its limited economic power and diverse interests translates into weak influence in many of the international fora where decisions are made. The African Union has to date made little progress in acquiring a common voice and mandate from member states to articulate a collective position, though some progress was made at WTO negotiations given the leading role of South Africa. In the climate change negotiations, African countries face the particular difficulty of very diverse interests, which render much harder the attainment of a common negotiating position. For example, several African countries have become major exporters of oil and gas, from which they receive a large share of government revenue. Others hope to benefit greatly from any payments mechanism for reduced emissions from deforestation and degradation. A few, such as South Africa, will need to invest significant sums in new energy systems that either allow carbon capture and storage from their coal-fired electricity generation, or enable a shift to low-carbon patterns of energy supply.

Climate change is not happening in a vacuum. Countries across the continent have been subject to many drivers of change, ranging from the continuing impact of the AIDS pandemic, worsening impoverishment in some regions, rising competition for scarce land and water resources, and ongoing conflicts and civil war. The poor majority tend to suffer worst from these forces both because of their vulnerability and because many governments do little to protect the weak. Women and women-headed households are particularly vulnerable to the combined impacts of food price rises, insecurity and changes to climate. The food price bubble of 2007/08 and the economic downturn from late 2008 onwards provide ample evidence of the subsidiary role in which poorer countries find themselves in times of crisis. While trillions of dollars were rapidly mobilized to bail out Western banks and financial sectors, many poor countries found themselves facing a freefall in commodity prices and migrants' remittances. Aid budgets are being cut and there has been a large reduction in foreign investment.

The rapid escalation in food and fuel prices in 2008, however, has also renewed interest in agriculture and food production. From a situation in which food prices had been falling in relative terms for the previous thirty years, there is now a growing belief that we should be prepared for a long-term rise in the price of food and other agricultural commodities. This has provoked an interest in countries that are highly dependent on food imports in seeking assured supplies from elsewhere, through acquisition of land for farming. A recent survey shows a rising trend in land-based investments, particularly in Africa, and anticipated future growth trends. The likely increase in commodity prices also makes acquisition of agricultural land an attractive option (Cotula et al. 2009). Such strategies raise a number of difficult issues, such as local people being moved off land they had relied on in favour of foreign investors, and risks to the sustainability of soil, water and biodiversity through large-scale mono-cropping of land (ibid.).

It is also likely that the costs of fossil fuel will rise over time to surpass the high of $145 a barrel reached in mid-2008. Oil and gas are such central elements in current economic systems, we will need a major increase in the oil price, or the carbon price, to help achieve the transformation needed in the pattern of energy use on which the world economy currently depends. But the transformation required also goes farther than just transport and energy. For example, our current patterns of agricultural production depend heavily on chemical fertilizer, pesticides and mechanization, while our food systems rely on transporting food long distances from farm to processor, via wholesale markets to retail outlets. The production of fertilizer is particularly energy intensive, as well as generating substantial greenhouse gases from its use in the form of nitrous oxides. Consequently, we need to harness nature in new ways, understanding and working with natural processes, building on agro-ecological principles rather than relying on chemical interventions. Equally, with cities now harbouring more than half of humanity, we need to redesign how human settlements work to ensure shelter, mobility, jobs and food in ways that minimize impacts on scarce resources and build resilience against future shocks.

Looking forward, African governments face several big issues in seeing how best they can address both the difficulties that climate change will bring and some of the new opportunities and funding streams stemming from the climate change negotiations. The

Clean Development Mechanism has provided few funds to date for African countries to access, because it was designed with only carbon in mind, rather than ease of access for small-scale producers of carbon. A new wave of finance will need to be designed which addresses the needs of poor countries and poor communities. A proposed payments mechanism for reduced emissions from deforestation and degradation has the potential to raise considerable funds to promote more sustainable forestry management. But again there are many questions as to who will benefit. Past history shows that the poor and vulnerable do not get a fair share of resources unless they can mobilize effectively and there is parallel pressure on the powerful to make decisions in favour of the many, not the few. In the context of the climate change negotiations, this means making sure that the voices of ordinary Africans – women, men, young, old, farmers and slum dwellers – are heard loud and clear as the policies and institutions for addressing this most challenging of global problems are designed.

Notes

2 Global climate change and Africa

1 CO_2 levels include other GHG expressed as CO_2 equivalents.

2 UNFCCC Essential Background, unfccc.int/essential_background/items/2877.php.

3 UNFCCC website, unfccc.int/kyoto_protocol/background/items/3145.php.

4 UNFCCC CDM statistics. CDM registered projects by region, cdm.unfccc.int/Statistics/Registration/.

5 ClimDev is an African development programme to integrate Climate Risk Management (CRM) into policy and decision processes throughout the continent. It is being implemented under the direction of the Joint African Union, Economic Commission for Africa and African Development Bank Secretariat with support from a number of sources.

3 Water

1 WaterAid website, www.wateraid.org/international/what_we_do/where_we_work/mali/examples_of_our_work_in_mali/default.asp.

2 Water scarcity = less than 1,000m³/person/year; water stress = between 1,000 and 1,700 m³/person/year. Source: UNEP, *Global Environment Outlook*, 1999.

3 iri.ldeo.columbia.edu/~bgordon/ITCZ.html.

4 en.wikipedia.org/wiki/El_Ni%C3%B1o-Southern_Oscillation.

5 Figures from IPCC (2007: ch. 9) and the Millennium Ecosystem Assessment report, Washington, DC: Island Press, 2005.

6 Department for Water Affairs and Forestry, Republic of South Africa, 2004, www.dwaf.gov.za/.

7 River Basin Initiative website, www.riverbasin.org/index.cfm?&menuid=100&parentid=87.

8 FAO, 'Irrigation potential in Africa: a basin approach', Natural Resources Management and Environment Department, www.fao.org/docrep/w4347e/w4347e0i.htm.

4 Food

1 Soaring food prices put further pressure on African agriculture. Director-General addresses the FAO Regional Conference for Africa 2008, www.fao.org/newsroom/en/news/2008/1000868/index.html.

2 See also www.fao.org/ES/ess/compendium_2006/list.asp.

3 Independent Online, 2008, www.iol.co.za/index.php?set_id=1&click_id=13 6&art_id=

nw20080208085024524 C692852. Source: East Africa Fine Coffee Association, www.eafca.org/index. asp.

4 See also FAO/Norway Government GCP/INT/648/NOR Cooperative Programme Field Report F-2 (En) GCP/INT/648/ NOR Fishcode Management, ftp. fao.org/docrep/fao/006/x1805e/ X1805E00.pdf.

5 go.worldbank.org/NKNK PX8FL0.

6 Examples include the UK government's Foresight Exercise on the Future of Food and Farming to 2050; and the Bill and Melinda Gates Foundation's programme of investment in African agriculture, including the Alliance for a Green Revolution in Africa (AGRA).

7 Hubert H. G. Savenije, 'The role of green water in food production in sub-Saharan Africa', FAO, www.fao.org/ag/agL/aglw/webpub/ greenwat.htm.

8 Livestock impacts on the environment: Spotlight 2006, www.fao.org/ag/magazine/ 0612sp1.htm.

5 Forests

1 From www.ens-newswire. com/ens/oct2005/2005-10-17-05. asp.

2 'The carbon cycle', Safe climate for business website, www.safeclimate.net/business/ understanding/carboncycle.php; 'The territorial biosphere's role in the carbon cycle', 'The carbon cycle: a simple explanation', Met

Office website, www.metoffice.gov. uk/research/hadleycentre/models/ carbon_cycle/into_terrest.html.

3 FAO, www.fao.org/ newsroom/en/news/2005/1000127/ index.html, accessed 18 February 2009.

4 Assuming a specific wood density of 0.5g dry matter/cm^3 and a carbon content of 0.5g carbon per gram of dry matter.

5 See also FAO, www.fao.org/ newsroom/en/news/2005/1000127/ index.html, accessed 19 February 2008.

6 www.policy powertools.org/ Tools/Engaging/docs/targeting_ livelihoods_evidence_tool_ english.pdf.

7 Ibid.

8 Based on average prices in 2003 of US$1 per kg of honey and US$2 per kg of beeswax (Mwakatobe and Mlingwa 2005).

9 World Resources Institute, Earth Trends website, earthtrends. wri.org/updates/node/303.

10 From www.cifor.cgiar.org/ publications/pdf_files/Books/ Restution-Africa_case/NTFP-Africa-case-part2.pdf.

6 Cities

1 This chapter draws on the work and the publications of the IIED's Human Settlements Group, especially the papers and case studies in Bicknell et al. (2009).

2 In some nations, official statistics suggest lower figures, but usually because poverty lines are set without taking account of the high cost of non-food needs

in these cities; see Satterthwaite (2004).

3 'Viumbe hai: African cities, ecosystems and biodiversity', United Nations Human Settlements Programme, hq.unhabitat.org/pmss/getPage. asp?page=bookView&book=2485.

4 wakabirigi.blogspot. com/2007/11/african-poor-to-share-on-gates-10m.html.

5 UNEP, www.unep.org/ Documents.Multilingual/. In early 2004, the British prime minister, Tony Blair, established the Commission for Africa. The seventeen members of the Commission, nine from Africa and all working in their individual and personal capacities, published their report, 'Our common interest', on 11 March 2005.

6 Practical Action, practical action.org/?id=commissionfor africa-response, accessed 14 March 2008.

7 World Bank, 'Adaptation to climate change in the Middle East and North Africa region', web.worldbank.org/WBSITE/ EXTERNAL/COUNTRIES/ MENAEXT/.

8 ICLEI Africa, www.iclei.org/ index.php?id=global-about-iclei, accessed 12 March 2008.

9 ICLEI Africa, www.iclei. org/index.php?id=689, accessed 12 March 2008.

10 This example is drawn from Roberts (2008a); see also Roberts (2008b: 4).

7 Climate change and conflict

1 Development Concept and Doctrine Centre, Directorate General of the UK Ministry of Defence, www.mod.uk/NR/gov.

2 Executive Office of the President: Office of Management and Budget, 'Federal climate change expenditures report to Congress', Washington, DC, May 2007; Steven M. Kosiak, 'Historical and projected funding for defense: presentation of the FY 2008 request in tables and charts', Center for Strategic and Budgetary Assessment, June 2007, in Pemberton (2008).

3 FPIF Policy Report, *Africa Policy Outlook*, 2008, www.fpif.org/ fpiftxt/4949.

4 nobelprize.org/nobel_prizes/ peace/laureates/2007/press.html.

5 Ibid.

6 Speech by Al Gore on the acceptance of the Nobel Peace Prize, Oslo, Norway, 10 December 2007.

7 There are already 10 million environmental refugees, and this is expected to rise to up to 50 million by the end of the decade; www.guardian.co.uk/environment/ 2005/oct/12/naturaldisasters. climatechange1.

8 FAO, www.fao.org/isfp/ country-information/ethiopia/en/.

9 GRAIN, 'The 2008 land grab for food and financial security', www.grain.org/go/landgrab.

8 Africa and the low-carbon economy

1 'Climate change will hit tourism revenues', www.travelweekly.

Notes

co.uk/Articles/2008/03/12/26935/
climate-change-will-hit-tourism-
revenues-says-deutsche.html,
12 March 2008.

9 *Looking forward*
  1 *Guardian*, 7 August 2008.
  2 Martin Parry, personal communication, 2009.

Bibliography

Adeyinka Sunday, O. and
    J. Taiwo Olalekan (2006) 'Lagos
    shoreline change pattern:
    1986–2002', *American-Eurasian
    Journal of Scientific Research*,
    1(1): 25–30.
African Biodiversity Network
    (2007) 'AGROfuels in Africa
    – the impacts on land, food
    and forests. Case Studies from
    Benin, Tanzania, Uganda and
    Zambia', July.
Agoumi, A. (2003) 'Vulnerability
    of North African countries to
    climatic changes, adaptation
    and implementation strategies
    for climatic change', IISD,
    www.iisd.org; Climate Change
    Knowledge Network, www.
    cckn.net.
Aina, D. and R. Andoh (2003)
    'Aspects of land-based pollu-
    tion of an African coastal
    megacity of Lagos', Paper pres-
    ented at the Diffuse Pollution
    Conference, Dublin.
Aina, T. A. (1995) 'Metropolitan
    Lagos: population growth
    and spatial expansion; city
    study', Background paper for
    the Global Report on Human
    Settlements.
Alden, C. (2007) *China in Africa*,
    London: Zed Books.
Allison, E. H., W. N. Adger,
    M. Badjeck, K. Brown, D. Con-
way, N. K. Dulvy, A. Halls,
    A. Perry and J. D. Reynolds
    (2005) 'Effects of climate
    change on the sustainability
    of capture and enhancement
    of fisheries important to the
    poor: analysis of the vulner-
    ability and adaptability of
    fisherfolk living in poverty',
    Fisheries Management Science
    Programme, Department for
    International Development
    Summary Report (Project no.
    R4778J), November, www.dfid.
    gov.uk/pubs/files/summary-
    climatechangefisheries.pdf.
Ashton, J. (2007) Speech to the
    'Climate change – the global
    security impact' conference,
    RUSI, London, 24 January.
Aty Sayed, M. A. (2008) 'Climate
    change will have various
    effects on water resources and
    water management in the Nile
    Basin', Paper presented at
    the 13th International Water
    Resources Association (IWRA)
    Congress, 2–4 September,
    Montpellier, France.
Barnaby, W. (2009) 'Do nations
    go to war over water?', *Nature*,
    458: 282–3.
Bates, S., Z. Wu, W. Kundzewicz
    and J. Palutikof (eds) (2008)
    Climate Change and Water,
    Geneva: IPCC Secretariat, June.

Bibliography

Belières, J. F. et al. (2002) 'What future for West Africa's family farms in a world market economy?', Issue Paper no. 113, London: IIED.

Bicknell, J. et al. (eds) (2009) *Adapting Cities to Climate Change: Understanding and Addressing the Development Challenges*, London: Earthscan.

Boko, M., I. Niang, A. Nyong and C. Vogel (2007) 'Impacts, adaptation and vulnerability', in IPCC, *Climate Change 2007 Synthesis Report. IPCC Fourth Assessment Report*, IPCC/UNEP, ch. 9.

Bonan, G. B. (2008) 'Forests and climate change: forcings, feedbacks and the climate benefits of forests', *Science*, 320(5882): 1444–9.

British Council (2004) 'A briefing on climate change and cities', Briefing Sheet 30, prepared for the British Council by the Tyndall Centre for Climate Change Research, December.

Brock, K. and N. Coulibaly (1998) 'Sustainable rural livelihoods in Mali', Research Report 35, Brighton: IDS.

Brown, O. and A. Crawford (2008) 'Assessing the security implications of climate change for West Africa', Country case studies of Ghana and Burkina Faso, IISD, Canada, www.iisd.org/pdf/2008/security_implications_west_africa.pdf.

Brown, O. et al. (2007) *International Affairs*, 83(6): 1141–54, www.iisd.org/pdf/2007/climate_security_threat_africa.pdf.

Campbell-Lendrum, D. and C. Corvalán (2007) 'Climate change and developing-country cities: implications for environmental health and equity', *Urban Health*, 84(suppl. 1): 109–17.

Canadell, J. G. and M. R. Raupach (2008) 'Managing forests for climate mitigation', *Science*, 320: 1456.

Capistrano, D. (2005) 'Storehouses and safety nets', *Our Planet*, 16(2): 30–31.

Chege, K. (2007) 'Biofuel: Africa's new oil?', Science and Development Network, 5 December, www.scidev.net.

Chege, N. (2001) 'Africa's non-timber forest economy', in M. Barany, A. L. Hammett, A. Sene and B. Amichev, 'Non-timber forest benefits and HIV/AIDS in sub-Saharan Africa', *Journal of Forestry*, December, www.sfp.forprod.vt.edu/pubs/ntfp_africa.pdf.

Christensen, J. H. and B. Hewitson (2007) 'Regional climate projections', Working Group 1, IPCC, *Climate Change 2007 Synthesis Report. IPCC Fourth Assessment Report*, IPCC/UNEP, ch. 11, www.ipcc.ch/pdf/assessment-report/ar4/wg1/ar4-wg1-chapter11.pdf.

CIA (2006) *The World Factbook*, Central Intelligence Agency, www.cia.gov/library/publications/ the-world-factbook/rankorder/2034rank.html.

Collier, P. (2007) *The Bottom Bil-*

lion: Why the Poorest Countries are Failing and What Can be Done About It, Oxford: OUP.

Collier, P. et al. (2008) *Beyond Greed and Grievance: Feasibility and Civil War*, Oxford: Oxford University Press.

Comenetz, J. and C. Caviedes (2003) 'Climate variability, political crises, and historical population displacements in Ethiopia', *Environmental Hazards*, 4: 113–27, www.vulnerabilitynet.org/OPMS/.

Cotula, L. (ed.) (2006) 'Land and water rights in the Sahel. Tenure challenges of improving access to water for agriculture', Issue Paper no. 139, London: IIED, March, www.iied.org/pubs/pdfs/12526IIED.pdf.

Cotula, L. and J. Mayers (2009) 'Tenure in REDD. Start-point or after-thought?', Paper prepared for the Prince of Wales's Rainforests Project, London: IIED.

Cotula, L., S. Vermeulen, R. Leonard and J. Keeley (2009) 'Land grab or development opportunity? New trends in government-partnered investment and land acquisition in Africa', London: IIED, FAO, IFAD.

Crosby, A., D. Murphy and J. Drexhage (2007) 'Market mechanisms for sustainable development: how do they fit in the various post-2012 climate efforts?', Development Dividend Project – Phase III, IISD, Canada, www.iisd.org/pdf/2007/market_mechanisms.pdf.

De Waal, A. (2007) 'Making sense of Darfur: is climate change the culprit for Darfur?', www.ssrc.org/blogs/darfur/2007.

Deininger, K. (2003) *Land Policies for Growth and Poverty Reduction*, Washington, DC: World Bank.

Derman, B., R. Odgaard and E. Sjaastad (2007) *Conflicts Over Land and Water in Africa*, Oxford: James Currey.

DfID (2007) 'Balancing the cost of food air miles: listening to trade and environmental concerns', www.dfid.gov.uk/news/files/foodmiles.asp.

Diamond, J. (2005) *Collapse: How Societies Choose to Fail or Survive*, New York: Viking Press.

Dossou, K. M. R. and B. Gléhouenou-Dossou (2007) 'The vulnerability to climate change of Cotonou (Benin): the rise in sea level', *Environment and Urbanization*, 19(1): 65–79, eau.sagepub.com/cgi/content/abstract/19/1/65.

Douglas, I., K. Alam, M. Maghenda, Y. McDonnell, L. McLean and J. Campbell (2008) 'Unjust waters: climate change, flooding and the urban poor in Africa', *Environment and Urbanization*, 20(1).

Dufey, A., S. Vermeulen and B. Vorley (2007) 'Biofuels: strategic choices for commodity dependent developing countries', London: IIED.

EarthTrends (2008) www.earthtrends.org/searchable_db/, Washington, DC: World Resources Institute.

Bibliography

159

Eid, H. M. et al. (2006) 'Assessing the economic impacts of climate change on agriculture in Egypt: a Ricardian approach', Discussion Paper no. 16, Special Series on Climate Change and Agriculture in Africa, Centre for Environmental Economics and Policy in Africa (CEEPA).

Eliasch Review (2008) *Climate Change – Financing Global Forests*, London: Earthscan.

El-Raey, M. (1997) 'Vulnerability assessment of the coastal zone of the Nile Delta of Egypt to the impact of sea level rise', *Ocean and Coastal Management*, 37(1): 29–40.

FAO (1999) *Lake Tanganyika Framework Fisheries Management*, Rome: Food and Agriculture Organization, April.

— (2005) 'Progress towards sustainable forest management', Global Forest Resources Assessment 2005, Forestry Paper 147.

— (2005/06) *Statistical Yearbook 2005–2006*, vol. 2/2, Country Profiles, www.fao.org/statistics/yearbook/vol_1_2/site_en.asp?page=cp.

— (2006) *Building Adaptive Capacity to Climate Change – policies to sustain livelihoods and fisheries*, New Directions in Fisheries – A Series of Policy Briefs on Development Issues, no. 8, Rome: Food and Agriculture Organization.

Fleshman, M. (2008) 'Africa struggles with soaring food prices', Africa Renewal, United Nations, 5 August 5, www.worldpress.org/Africa/3217.cfm.

Garside, B., J. MacGregor and B. Vorley (2007) 'Miles better? How "fair miles" stack up in the sustainable supermarket', *Sustainable Development Opinion*, London: IIED, December, www.iied.org/pubs/pdfs/17024IIED.pdf.

Global Carbon Project (2008) 'Global warming may reduce carbon sink capacity in Northern forests', *Science Daily*, 3 January.

Hansen, L. J., J. L. Biringer and J. R. Hoffman (eds) (2003) 'Buying time: a user's manual for building resistance and resilience to climate change in natural systems', WWF Climate Change Programme.

Hare, B. (2008) 'Science of climate change. Breaking the climate deadlock', Climate Group briefing paper.

Homer-Dixon, T. F. (2009) *Environment, Scarcity and Violence*, Princeton, NJ: Princeton University Press.

Huq, S. et al. (2007) 'Editorial: reducing risks to cities from disasters and climate change', *Environment and Urbanization*, 19: 3–15.

IAASTD (2009) 'Agriculture at a crossroads', International Assessment of Agricultural Knowledge, Science and Technology for Development, Washington, DC: Island Press.

ICRISAT (2008) 'Sweet sorghum: a new smart biofuel crop that ensures food security', www. icrisat.org/Media/2008/media6. htm.

IEA (2004) *World Energy Outlook*, Paris: International Energy Agency, 2004.

IIED (2009) 'AdMit: Responsible choice in the carbon market', London.

IPCC (2007) *Climate Change 2007 Synthesis Report. IPCC Fourth Assessment Report*, IPCC/UNEP.

IRIN (2007) 'Mozambique: no lift-off for biofuels yet', *IRIN News*, www.ecc-platform. org/index.php?option=com_ content&task=view&id=1208.

Jallow, B. P. and T. Downing (2007) 'NAPAs: priorities to policies', *Tiempo: A Bulletin on Climate and Development*, 65, October, www.cru.uea.ac.uk/ tiempo/portal/archive/pdf/ tiempo65low.pdf.

James, C. (2004) 'Preview: global status of commercialized biotech/GM crops: 2004', ISAAA Briefs no. 32, Ithaca, NY: ISAAA.

Jorgenson, S. E., G. Ntakimazi and S. Kayombo (2006) 'Lake Tanganyika experience and lessons learned', World Bank Brief, www.ilec.or.jp/ eg/lbmi/reports/22_Lake_ Tanganyika_27February2006. pdf.

Juma, C. and I. Serageldin (2007) 'Freedom to innovate. Biotechnology in Africa's development', AU high-level panel, Addis Ababa.

Kambewa, P., B. Mataya, K. Sichinga and T. Johnson (2007) 'Charcoal: the reality – a study of charcoal consumption, trade and production in Malawi', Small and Medium Forestry Enterprise Series no. 21, London: IIED.

Kanji, N. et al. (2006) 'Can land registration serve poor and marginalised groups?' London: IIED.

Kanninen, M., D. Murdiyarso, F. Seymour, A. Angelsen, S. Wunder and L. German (2007) 'Do trees grow on money? The implications of deforestation research for policies to promote REDD', Center for International Forestry Research (CIFOR), www.cifor. cgiar.org/Publications/Detail. htm?pid=2347.

Larkin, N. K. and D. E. Harrison (2002) 'ENSO warm and cold event life cycles: ocean surface anomaly patterns, their symmetries, asymmetries and implications', *Journal of Climate*, 15(10): 1118–40.

Lavigne-Delville, P. et al. (2002) 'Negotiating access to land in West Africa: a synthesis of findings from research on derived rights to land', London: IIED, GRET, IRD.

Le Billon, P. (2007) 'Geographies of war: perspectives on "resource wars"', *Geography Compass*, 1/2: 163–82, www. blackwell-synergy.com/ doi/full/10.1111/j.1749-8198.2007.00010.x.

Leach, M. and J. Fairhead (1997) 'Webs of power: forest loss in Guinea', in R. Rillo and R. L. Sirrat (eds), *Discourses of Development*, Oxford: Berg Press.

McGranahan, G., D. Balk and B. Anderson (2007) 'The rising tide: assessing the risks of climate change and human settlements in low-elevation coastal zones', *Environment and Urbanization*, 19(1): 17–37.

MacGregor, J. and B. Vorley (2006) 'Fair miles? The concept of "food miles" through a sustainable development lens', *Sustainable Development Opinion*, London: IIED.

McGregor, G. R., M. Pelling, T. Wolf and S. Gosling (2007) 'The social impacts of heat waves', Environment Agency Science Report – SC20061/SR6, August.

Macqueen, D. and S. Vermeulen (2006) 'Climate change and forest resilience', *Sustainable Development Opinion*, London: IIED.

Meadows, D. H. et al. (1972) *The Limits of Growth. A Report for the Club of Rome's Project on the Predicament of Mankind*, New York: Universe Books.

Morris, M. et al. (2007) *Fertiliser Use in African Agriculture*, Washington, DC: World Bank.

Moyo, D. (2009) *Dead Aid*, London: Allen Lane.

Muller, A. and D. Mitlin (2007) 'Securing inclusion: strategies for community empowerment and state redistribution', *Environment and Urbanization*, 19(2): 425–39.

Muller, M. (2007) 'Adapting to climate change: water management for urban resilience', *Environment and Urbanization*, 19(1): 99–113.

Mwakatobe, A. and C. Mlingwa (2005) 'The status of Tanzanian honey trade – domestic and international markets', Tanzania Wildlife Research Institute, www.tanzaniagateway.org/docs/the_status_of_tanzanian_honey_trade_markets_nov2--6.pdf.

Nabuurs, G. J. et al. (2007) 'Forestry', in *Climate Change 2007 Synthesis Report. IPCC Fourth Assessment Report*, Working Group III, IPCC/UNEP.

NRC (1981) *Effects of Environment on Nutrient Requirements of Domestic Animals*, Washington, DC: National Academy Press.

Nwafor, J. C. (1986) 'Physical environment, decision-making and land use development in Metropolitan Lagos', *Geo-Journal*, 12(4): 433–42.

ODI (2006) 'Can tourism help reduce poverty in Africa?', www.sarpn.org.za/documents/d0001956/ODI_March06_Tourism.pdf.

Offerle, B., P. Jonsson, I. Eliasson and C. S. Grimmond (2005) 'Urban modification of the surface energy balance in the West African Sahel: Ouagadougou, Burkina Faso', *Journal of Climate*, 18(19): 3983,ams.allenpress. com/

perlserv/?request= get-abstract& doi=10.1175%2 FJCLI3520.1.

Oksanen, T. (2007) 'Strengthening forest law enforcement and governance: World Bank approach and experience', Washington, DC: World Bank.

Oxfam (2007) 'Biofuelling poverty – EU plans could be disastrous for poor people', www.oxfam. org.uk/applications/blogs/press office/2007/11/biofuelling_ poverty_eu_plans_c.html.

— (2008) *Shooting Down the MDGs. How irresponsible arms transfers undermine development goals*, Oxford.

Paeth, H. K., K. Born, R. Podzuin and D. E. Jacob (2005) 'Regional dynamical downscaling over West Africa: model evaluation and comparison of wet and dry years', *Meteorologische Zeitschrift*, 14(3): 349–67, www.mad.zmaw.de/ fileadmin/extern/Publications/ Regional_dynamical.pdf.

Pelling, M. (2007) 'Urbanization and disaster risk', Panel contribution to the Population-Environment Research Network Cyberseminar on Population and Natural Hazards, November, www.populationenvironment research.org/seminars.jsp.

Pemberton, M. (2008) 'The budgets compared: military vs. climate security', *Foreign Policy in Focus*, Institute for Policy Studies, January, www.fpif.org/ fpiftxt/4933.

Pernetta, J. (2004) 'Impacts of climate change on ecosystems and species', *Terrestrial Ecosystems*, pp. 89–91.

Petheram, L., B. Campbell, C. Marunda, D. Tiveau and S. Shackleton (2006) 'The wealth of the dry forests: can sound forest management contribute to the Millennium Development Goals in sub-Saharan Africa?', Forest Livelihood Briefs no. 5, CIFOR, October.

Petit, R. J., F. Sheng Hu and C. W. Dick (2008) 'Forests of the past: a window to future changes', *Science*, 320(5882): 1450–52.

Pile, R., T. Wrigley and C. Green (2008) 'Dangerous assumptions', *Nature*, 452: 531–2.

Pimbert, M. (2009) 'Towards food sovereignty. Reclaiming autonomous food systems', London: IIED.

Potts, Deborah (2009) 'The slowing of sub-Saharan Africa's urbanization: evidence and implications for urban livelihoods', *Environment and Urbanization*, 21(1).

Prince's Rainforests Project (2008) 'A plan for emergency funding', Consultative document, London: Clarence House, December.

Priscoli, J. Delli (1998) 'Water and civilization: reframing the debate on water and conflict', Paper presented at the IXth World Water Congress, 1–6 September 1997, Montreal,

Canada, in A. T. Wolf, 'Conflict and cooperation along international waterways', *Water Policy*, 1(2): 251–65, www.transboundarywaters.orst.edu/publications/conflict_coop/.

Rawls, J. (1971) *A Theory of Justice*, Cambridge, MA: Belknap.

Reid, H. and D. Satterthwaite (2007) 'Climate change and cities: why urban agendas are central to adaptation and mitigation', IIED, December, www.iied.org/pubs/display.php?o=17025IIED&n= 1&l=45 &a=Dpercent20Satterthwaite.

Reij, C. (2008) *Proposal: Regreening the Sahel*, Free University, Amsterdam.

Reij, C., I. Scoones and C. Toulmin (1996) *Sustaining the Soil*, London: Earthscan.

Reij, C., G. Tappan and A. Belemvire (2005) 'Changing land management practices and vegetation on the Central Plateau of Burkina Faso (1968–2002)', *Journal of Arid Environments*, 63: 642–59.

Republic of Kenya (2007) *First National Communication of Kenya to the Conference of Parties to the United Nations Framework Convention on Climate Change*, Ministry of Environment and Natural Resources, Nairobi, 2002, in IPCC, *Climate Change 2007 Synthesis Report. IPCC Fourth Assessment Report*, Working Group II, ch. 9.4, IPCC/UNEP.

Richards, P. (2006) *No Peace, No War: An Anthropology of Contemporary Armed Conflicts*, Oxford: James Currey.

— (2008) 'Against ethnicity – some anthropological arguments', Paper presented at the Conference on Rethinking Ethnicity and Ethnic Strife: Multidisciplinary Perspectives, European University, Budapest, 25–27 September.

Roberts, D. (2008a) 'Thinking globally, acting locally – institutionalizing climate change at the local government level in Durban, South Africa', *Environment and Urbanization*, 20(2): 521–38.

— (2008b) 'Durban adapts to climate change', *Climate Change and Cities*, id21 Insights 71, Brighton: id21 and IDS.

Rubyogo, J. C. and L. Sperling (2009) 'Developing seed systems in Africa', in I. Scoones and J. Thompson (eds), *Farmer First Revisited*, Rugby: Practical Action.

Saastamoinen, O. (2003) 'Forests and poverty reduction: the first UNEP/University of Joensuu symposium on challenges to sustainable development', University of Joensuu, 12 May, www.joensuu.fi/unep/pages/sym_saastamoinen.htm.

Santilli, M., P. Moutinho, S. Schwartzman, D. Nepstad, L. Curran and C. Nobre (2005) 'Tropical deforestation and the Kyoto Protocol, an editorial essay', *Climate Change*, 71: 267–76.

Satterthwaite, D. (2004) 'The

under-estimation of urban poverty in low- and middle-income nations', Working Paper no. 14 on Poverty Reduction in Urban Areas, London: IIED.

Satterthwaite, D., S. Huq, H. Reid, M. Pelling and P. Romero Lankao (2007) 'Adapting to climate change in urban areas: the possibilities and constraints in low- and middle-income nations', London: IIED, October, www.iied.org/pubs/pdfs/10549IIED.pdf.

Saunders, J. (2007) 'Reduced emissions from avoided deforestation and degradation (REDD) and forest governance', www.illegal-logging.info/.

Schwartz, P. and D. Randall (2003) *An Abrupt Climate Change Scenario and Its Implications for United States National Security*, New York: Environmental Defense, October, www.edf.org/documents/3566_Abrupt ClimateChange.pdf.

Scoones, I. et al. (1992) *The Hidden Harvest: Wild foods and agricultural systems*, London: IIED.

Skinner, J. (2009) 'Where every drop counts: tackling rural Africa's water crisis', Briefing Paper, London: IIED.

Smith, D. and J. Vivekananda (2007) *A Climate of Conflict: The Links Between Climate Change, Peace and War*, London: International Alert, www.international-alert.org/publications/322.php.

Stern, N. (2006) *Stern Review on the Economics of Climate Change*, London: HM Treasury, www.hm-treasury.gov.uk/independent_reviews/stern_review_economics_climate_change/stern _review_report.cfm, and Cambridge: Cambridge University Press, 2007.

— (2009) *A Blueprint for a Safer Planet: How to Manage Climate Change and Create a New Era of Progress and Prosperity*, Oxford: Bodley Head.

Stewart, F. (2007) 'How does conflict undermine human development?', http://hdr.undp.org/nhdr.

Tacoli, C. (2007) 'Migration and adaptation to climate change', Sustainable Development Opinion, IIED, November, www.iied.org/pubs/pdfs/17020IIED.pdf.

Tennigkeit, T. and A. Wilkes (2008) *Carbon Finance in Rangelands*, Kunming, China: World Agroforestry Centre.

Thornton, P. K. et al. (2006) 'Mapping climate vulnerability and poverty in Africa', Report to the Department for International Development, London, 2006, and *African Journal of Agricultural and Resource Economics*, 2(1), March 2008.

Toulmin, C. and B. Gueye (2003) 'Transformations in West African agriculture and the role of family farms', Issue Paper no. 123, London: IIED.

Toulmin, C. and J. Quan (2000) 'Evolving land rights, policy

and tenure', London: DfID/
IIED/NRI.

UN (2008) *The State of African
Cities*, Nairobi: UN-HABITAT.

UNDP (2007/08) *Human Development Report 2007/2008*, New
York: UN Development Pro-
gramme.

UNEP (2005) 'Hydropolitical
vulnerability and resilience
– Africa', United Nations Environment Programme, www.
acwr.co.za/pdf_files/03.pdf.

UNFPA (2007) 'Report – state of
the world population 2007.
Unleashing the potential of
urban growth', www.unfpa.org/
swp/2007/english/introduction.
html.

URT (United Republic of Tanzania) (2001) Rural Development Strategy, Final Draft,
Prime Minister's Office.

— (2002) 'Prudent exploitation of
tourism potential for wealth
creation and poverty reduction', Keynote address by the
president of the United Republic of Tanzania, His Excellency
Benjamin William Mkapa, at
the Tanzania Tourism Investment Forum, Dar es Salaam:
Government Printer.

Vermeulen, S. (2006) 'Forest and
social resilience to climate
change', Report of an informal
meeting between IIED and
partners, Nairobi, 15 November.

Viner, D. and M. Agnew (1999)
'Climate change and its
impacts on tourism', Report
prepared for WWF-UK by

Climatic Research Unit,
University of East Anglia, July,
www.wwf.org.uk/filelibrary/pdf/
tourism_and_cc_full.pdf.

Von Braun, J. (2007) 'When food
makes fuel: the promises and
challenges of biofuels', Keynote address, Biofuels, Energy
and Agriculture, International
Food Policy Research Institute,
Crawford Fund Annual Conference, Australia, 15 August,
www.ifpri.org/pubs/speeches/
vonbraun/2007jvbcrawford
keynote.pdf.

Von Braun, J. and R. Meinzen-Dick
(2009) '"Land grabbing" by
foreign investors in developing
countries: risks and opportunities', IFPRI Policy Brief,
Washington, DC.

Wanyoike, F. and K. M. Rich (2007)
'Socio-economic impacts of
the Rift Valley fever outbreak
in Kenya: a case study of
the North-Eastern Province
livestock marketing chain',
Nairobi: ILRI.

Ward, B. and R. Dubos (1972)
Only One Earth, London: André
Deutsch.

WCD (2000) *Dams and Development. A new framework for
decision-making. The report of
the World Commission on Dams*,
London: Earthscan, 2000.

WHO/UNICEF (2008) 'Progress on
drinking water and sanitation:
special focus on sanitation',
World Health Organization
and United Nations Children's
Fund Joint Monitoring Programme for Water Supply and

Sanitation (JMP), New York/
Geneva: UNICEF/WHO.

Wilbanks, T. and P. Romero
Lankao (2007) 'Industry, settle-
ment, and society', in IPCC,
*Climate Change 2007 Synthesis
Report. IPCC Fourth Assessment
Report*, IPCC/UNEP, ch. 7.

Williams, C. A., N. P. Hanan,
J. C. Neff, R. J. Scholes,
J. A. Berry, A. S. Denning and
D. F. Baker (2007) 'Africa and
the global carbon cycle review',
*Carbon Balance and Manage-
ment*, 2(3), www.cbmjournal.
com/content/2/1/3.

Witsenburg, K. and A. W. Roba
(2007) 'The use and management of water sources in
Kenya's drylands: is there a link
between scarcity and violent
conflicts?', in B. Derman, R. Odgaard and E. Sjaastad (2007)
*Conflicts over Land and Water in
Africa*, Oxford: James Currey.

World Bank (2004) *Strengthening
Forest Law Enforcement and
Governance*, Washington, DC:
World Bank.

— (2007) 'Biofuels: the promise
and the risks', *World Development Report 2008: Agriculture
for Development*, Washington,
DC: World Bank.

— (2008) *World Development
Report 2008: Agriculture for
Development*, Washington, DC:
World Bank.

Index

Index